Leon Trotsky on Black Nationalism & Self-Determination

Leon Trotsky in Coyoacán, Mexico

Leon Trotsky on Black Nationalism & Self-Determination

PATHFINDER PRESS
New York and Toronto

Edited by George Breitman

Copyright © 1967 by Merit Publishers
Copyright © 1978 by Pathfinder Press
All rights reserved
Library of Congress catalog card no. 78-59358
ISBN: cloth 87348-556-4 • paper 87348-557-2
Manufactured in the United States of America

First edition 1967
Second edition 1978

Published in the United States by
Pathfinder Press, 410 West St., New York, N.Y. 10014,
and simultaneously in Canada by Pathfinder Press, Ltd.,
25 Bulwer St., Toronto, Ontario

Contents

Preface to the Second Edition

The purpose of *Leon Trotsky on Black Nationalism and Self-Determination* was to reprint the great Russian revolutionary's major statements on the subject, made in the course of four discussions he held with American comrades during the last decade of his life, and two resolutions (Appendix A) that were adopted, under the influence of these discussions, at the 1939 convention of the Socialist Workers Party. The first edition, published in 1967, had four printings and greater sales in the United States than any other Trotsky compilation in the last decade.

Minor changes have been made in this second edition. The 1933 discussion in Prinkipo was held not in English, as we had supposed, but in German, and for this edition we have retranslated Trotsky's remarks from the German transcript, by permission of the Harvard College Library. We have also been able to check the original transcripts of the three Coyoacán discussions in 1939, held in English, and to correct a few passages in them, by permission of the Library of Social History in New York. And we have added an excerpt to the selection of Trotsky comments on nationalism and racial oppression (Appendix B).

Our editorial introductions, written in 1967, have been corrected in a few places and expanded in others. Terminology and spelling used in the 1930s or 1960s have not been revised to conform to present usage. The number of editorial footnotes has been increased, and an index has been added.

The Editor
October 1977

In Prinkipo, 1933: Trotsky (upper left); his American visitor Arne Swabeck (upper center); and Trotsky's secretaries Pierre Frank (upper right), Jean van Heijenoort (lower left), and Rudolf Klement (lower right).

Editorial Introduction

On April 8, 1964, James Wechsler, editor of the liberal *New York Post,* attended a meeting in midtown Manhattan where Malcolm X spoke on "The Black Revolution." It was the first of three meetings under the sponsorship of the Militant Labor Forum at which Malcolm spoke during the last year of his life, following his break with the Black Muslims. Wechsler described the forum as "a unit of the Socialist Workers Party (the continuing modern manifestation of what old radicals define as 'Trotskyism')" and then went on to say: "There was an intriguing aspect of the auspices of the meeting. It was hard to believe that Leon Trotsky had ever anticipated such an alliance would be welded in his memory. . . ." ("The Cult of Malcolm X," *Progressive,* June 1964.)

Wechsler found it "hard to believe that Leon Trotsky had ever anticipated such an alliance," because, despite the air of knowingness he sought to convey, he was quite ignorant of what Trotsky thought about the American Negro struggle. Malcolm, the self-educated man, knew more than the politically sophisticated Wechsler about Trotsky's views on the Negro; he knew that they were revolutionary, not liberal, because he had read, in 1963, the text of Trotsky's four discussions with his American comrades.

The present collection will show, among other things, what Trotsky's attitude would have been to Malcolm and what Malcolm represented. It fills the most important gap in the otherwise splendid anthology of Trotsky's thought, *The Age of Permanent Revolution,* edited by Isaac Deutscher with the assistance of George Novack (Dell,

9

1964). Since Trotsky's statements were made more than a quarter of a century ago, under circumstances with which most readers today are not familiar, a certain amount of background information is necessary.

Until the 1920s the American radical movement had little to its credit in connection with the Negro struggle. As James P. Cannon, a founder of the Communist Party and later a founder of the Socialist Workers Party, puts it, American radicals, including the new Communist Party, "had nothing to start with on the Negro question but an inadequate *theory,* a false or indifferent *attitude* and the adherence of a few individual Negroes of radical or revolutionary bent." The inadequate theory, from which the attitude and lack of influence followed, was that the oppression of the Negro people was purely and simply "an economic problem, part of the struggle between the workers and capitalists; nothing could be done about the special problems of discrimination and inequality this side of socialism." In practice, Cannon says, this turned out to be "a formula for inaction on the Negro front, and—incidentally—a convenient shield for the dormant racial prejudices of the white radicals themselves" (*The First Ten Years of American Communism,* Lyle Stuart, 1962, republished by Pathfinder, 1973).

The Russian revolution of 1917 changed this, as so many other things. Cannon says:

> Even before the First World War and the Russian Revolution, Lenin and the Bolsheviks were distinguished from all other tendencies in the international socialist and labor movement by their concern with the problems of oppressed nations and national minorities, and affirmative support of their struggles for freedom, independence and the right of self-determination. . . .
>
> After November, 1917 this new doctrine—with special emphasis on the Negroes—began to be transmitted to the American communist movement with the authority of the Russian Revolution behind it. The Russians in the Comintern started on the American communists with the harsh, insistent demand that they shake off their unspoken preju-

dices, pay attention to the special problems and grievances of the American Negroes, go to work among them, and champion their cause in the white community.

It took time for the Americans, raised in a different tradition, to assimilate the new Leninist doctrine. But the Russians followed up year after year, piling up the arguments and increasing the pressure. . . .

And so, Cannon says, American Marxists finally learned, "slowly and painfully," to "change their *attitude;* to assimilate the new theory of the Negro question as a *special* question of doubly-exploited second-class citizens, requiring a program of special demands as part of the overall program—and to start doing something about it."

Thus serious Marxist attention to the Negro struggle, and serious Marxist attempts to construct a suitable theory to guide action in that struggle, began, like most other good things in America, through "outside" influence. They probably could not have begun any other way in a country where racism is so pervasive that not even revolutionists are immune to its more subtle poisons. Nor was this the last time that American Marxists concerned with the Negro struggle received healthy guidance and correction from outside, that is, international revolutionary, sources.

In 1928 the Communist Party expelled Cannon and others who opposed the revisions of Marxism and the bureaucratic practices of the Stalinist faction that had gained dominance in the Communist International. The expelled group organized itself as the Communist League of America (CLA), and affiliated itself to the International Left Opposition, a faction of the Communist International that was organized in 1930 and led by Trotsky. By 1929, when the CLA held its first national conference, Trotsky had made contact with his American cothinkers, and from Turkey, where he had been exiled by the Stalinist bureaucracy, he sent a letter in April expressing his views on "Tasks of the American Opposition." There were many things he wanted to tell his comrades in the United States, but he did not fail to include a warning of their need to resist "aristocratic prejudices" and to find a way to the most exploited sections of society, "beginning with the Negro":

> The trade union bureaucrats, like the bureaucrats of pseudo-communism, live in an atmosphere of aristocratic prejudices of the upper strata of the workers. It would be tragic if the Oppositionists were infected even in the slightest degree with these qualities. We must not only reject and condemn these prejudices; we must burn them out of our consciousness to the last trace. We must find the road to the most unprivileged and downtrodden strata of the proletariat, beginning with the Negroes, whom capitalist society has converted into pariahs, and who must learn to see in us their brothers. And this depends entirely upon our energy and devotion to this work [*Militant*, May 1, 1929, reprinted in *Writings of Leon Trotsky (1929)*, Pathfinder, 1975].

During its first five years the Communist League of America considered itself to be and functioned as a faction of the Communist Party. Instead of trying to establish a new party in opposition to the CP, it sought to reform the CP—to get it to change its wrong policies. Its own activities were largely determined, defined, and limited by this aim. Where it thought the CP's policies and actions correct, it supported them; where it thought them wrong, it criticized and opposed them. In the area of the Negro struggle the differences between the two organizations were, for the most part, over minor and tactical questions, and did not figure prominently in the CLA's program or literature.

The chief exception was the position on "self-determination for the Black Belt" adopted by the Communist International in 1928 and then accepted by the American Communist Party. Since there has been so much confusion about this question, it may help to discuss the general concept of self-determination by itself before examining the CP's specific use of it.

The general concept, as developed by Lenin and the Russian Bolsheviks, referred to the right of oppressed nations, nationalities, and minorities to decide their destinies for themselves, including the right to separate into a nation of their own. Nobody who strove to be a Leninist questioned this general concept. The question at issue was: Did this concept apply to the black people in the United States, and if so, how?

Lenin himself evidently thought it applied. In his "Preliminary Draft of Theses on the National and Colonial Questions," written for the Second Congress of the Communist International in 1920, he included American Negroes among the oppressed minorities of the world when he said:

> all Communist parties should render direct aid to the revolutionary movements among the dependent and underprivileged nations (for example, Ireland, the American Negroes, etc.) and in the colonies [*Collected Works,* vol. 31, p. 148].*

But while Lenin apparently thought that the general right of self-determination applied to American Negroes, he did not go beyond that conclusion and propose slogans or tactics flowing from this general right. This may have been because he lacked close acquaintance with the history, conditions, moods, and psychology of the Negro people, or it may have been for other reasons. In any case, neither in 1920 nor in the remaining four years of his life did he attempt to indicate *how* he thought the general right of self-determination should be concretized and utilized in the American Negro struggle. Neither did the Communist International nor the American Communist Party, which continued to stress the fight for equality inside American society.

---

*Theodore Draper asserts that a more accurate translation of this passage is less clear-cut: "Communist parties must give direct support to the revolutionary movements among the dependent nations and those without equal rights (e.g., in Ireland, among the American Negroes, etc.) and in the colonies" (*American Communism and Soviet Russia,* Viking, 1960, p. 337). But Lenin was unambiguous when he said in 1917 that Negroes in the United States "should be classed as an oppressed nation" (*Collected Works,* vol. 23, p. 275).

After Lenin's death, the Communist International and the Soviet Union were taken over by a privileged bureaucratic caste, headed by Stalin, which professed allegiance to Marxism and Leninism but which could not and would not pursue a genuinely Marxist and Leninist policy. In 1928, the leaders of this group* decided that the Negro people in the United States conformed to Stalin's definition of a nation and therefore should fight not only for equality in the North and South but for the "right of self-determination in the South." Two years later, in another Communist International resolution, they decreed that "self-determination" must be the "chief slogan" in the South. The American CP spelled it out in November 1928: "The Communists Are For a Black Republic," and soon was busy publishing maps which showed just where the boundaries of this republic would be in the South.

The American CP was never given a chance even to discuss this position before it was decided on in Moscow; that was a sign of how bureaucratic the Communist International had become. Worse yet was the fact that the position was adopted in total disregard of the twelve million black people in the United States. The very term "self-determination" implies the right of an oppressed group—that is, those most directly affected—to decide for themselves what they want, and how, and when. But the Stalinist bureaucrats, who had already begun to destroy workers' democracy in the Soviet Union, took it upon themselves to "determine" for the Negro people what their slogans and goals should be. Did the Negroes *want* a separate nation? If they did, did they *want* it to be located in the South? Never mind—the Stalinists knew what was best, like father. A more arbitrary caricature of the right of self-determination has never been seen. It is not surprising that the American CP never attracted many Negroes with this position, despite the various modifications they made in it, and that its recruitment of Negroes during the 1930s

---

*Theodore Draper is probably right in tracing the initiating role to Stalin himself (ibid., pp. 342-45).

took place despite this position, and because of the CP's vigorous activities in behalf of equal rights.*

It was and is easy, and conventional, to condemn the way the Stalinists applied or misapplied the general concept of self-determination to the situation of the Negro people. Reformists and liberals, white and black, have long had a field day with this, and with their taunts that the CP was promoting its own brand of "Negro segregation." But Marxists and revolutionists could not be content merely with rejecting the CP caricature; sooner or later they had to confront the issue itself: Were the Negro people entitled to exercise the right of self-determination, including the right of separation (in whatever way they chose)? And what should Marxists say and do about the decision the Negro people made?

The leaders of the CLA were troubled by this problem and, at the beginning, divided over it. The draft of their original platform, which was presented to the CLA's founding conference in 1929, stated:

> The Negro question is also a national question, and the Party must raise the slogan of the right of self-determination for the Negroes. The effectiveness of this

---

*Space does not permit following the numerous twists and turns in the application of this position by Moscow and the American CP. Whatever the intention may have been at the start, their opportunism and cynicism became obvious after a few years. Whenever the Soviet bureaucracy wanted to exert extra pressure on the U.S. government, it shoved the self-determination slogan to the fore (for example, in Stalin's ultraleft "third period," 1928-34, and at the start of the cold war after World War II). Whenever it saw the possibility of a class-collaborationist deal with Washington (the "People's Front" period of 1935-39 and the more recent "peaceful coexistence" period), the self-determination slogan was shelved or dumped. It was dropped altogether at the 1959 CP convention. These shifts—now in favor, now against— had nothing to do with the needs or wishes of the Negro people, who were never consulted or heeded; they derived from the foreign policy interests and diplomatic maneuvers of the Soviet bureaucracy.

slogan is enhanced by the fact that there are scores of
contiguous counties in the South where the Negro population is in the majority, and it is there that they suffer the
most violent persecution and discrimination. . . . The Party
must at the same time decisively reject the false slogan of a
"Negro Soviet Republic in the South" at this time. . . . This
theory is still being propagated in the Party press and in
official Party literature despite its rejection even at the
Sixth Congress of the Comintern ["Platform of the Communist Opposition," *Militant,* February 15, 1929].

This draft formulation was defended by Cannon, who
had been a delegate to the Sixth Congress in 1928 and said
he had learned a great deal from the discussions of the
subject at the sessions of the congress's program commission. But the delegates at the CLA conference decided to
delete these passages from their platform on the ground
that the whole question required further information and
consideration, and Cannon agreed that the decision to
postpone final action was justified. The point was deferred
to the CLA's second national conference in 1931, but the
leaders still had no answers then.

Like the CP, the CLA had gone beyond the old pre–World
War I radical tradition and recognized the need to formulate a program against racial oppression. But unlike the
CP after 1928, the CLA leaders did not see "national"
aspects in the Negro struggle. They were aware that in the
early 1920s Marcus Garvey, preaching separatism and a
return to Africa, had rallied the biggest black mass
movement the country had ever known, but they were also
aware that this movement had fallen apart after its
leader's imprisonment and deportation, and they saw little
evidence among the Negro people of what today would be
called black nationalism. They denied that they contested
the right of Negroes to self-determination, but they did not
believe that it was the issue around which Negroes could
be mobilized for struggle, and they feared that self-
determinationist slogans (not just the CP's, but any) would
do harm rather than good; hence they were reluctant to
express their support of the right which they said they did
not contest.

But they were not certain, and had not reached the point of formulating a position or program in writing. So when an opportunity arose early in 1933 for Arne Swabeck, one of the CLA leaders, to visit Trotsky in Prinkipo, Turkey, one of the subjects Swabeck was asked to discuss with Trotsky was "The Negro Question in America." The discussion was held in German on February 28, 1933, and a translation of the summary transcript of the discussion is the first part of the present collection.

Trotsky had spent only a few weeks in the United States (in 1917), and although he read and understood English, he did not speak it well. As he himself stated in the discussion, he had never studied American race relations, and the views he presented were based only upon "general considerations" (which he had expounded earlier in *The History of the Russian Revolution,* vol. 3, chapter 2, "The Problem of Nationalities"), and "upon the arguments brought forward by the American comrades" (which he found insufficient or dangerously wrong). Despite these reservations, and despite his recognition that whether the Negroes become a nation "is a question of their consciousness, that is, what they desire and what they strive for," Trotsky said he could see "no reason why we should not advance the demand for 'self-determination,'" and that on this question he would "rather lean toward the standpoint" of the CP than that of the CLA.* To the argument that Negroes were not demanding self-determination he responded, that is "of course for the same reason that the white workers do not yet advance the slogan of the dictatorship of the proletariat. The Negroes have not yet got it into their heads that they dare to carve out a piece of the great and mighty States for themselves." He plainly expected the Negroes to get this idea into their heads as much as he expected the white workers to become revolutionary.

---

*The impression left by Theodore Draper in *American Communism and Soviet Russia* (p. 510) that Trotsky arrived at a pro–self-determination position only in 1939 is therefore erroneous. He corrected this in a later book, *The Rediscovery of Black Nationalism* (Viking, 1970).

Trotsky's remarks were not confined to the self-determination controversy. To show his American comrades how he thought revolutionists should react to the oppression of the Negroes, he denounced the prejudiced white workers in more scathing, more bitter terms than any American Marxist, black or white, had ever done; even in his Black Muslim days Malcolm X never used harsher language. It is unrealistic, he said, to expect the Negro to reach "a class point of view" ahead of the white worker; that can happen "only when the white worker is educated" (class-conscious and anticapitalist), and understands his duty to his black brother. Despite that, the oppression of the Negroes is such that they can become revolutionary ahead of the white workers, furnish the vanguard of the revolution, and fight better for a new society than the white workers. But, he added, for that to happen, the revolutionary party must carry on "an uncompromising merciless struggle not against the supposed national prepossessions [black nationalism] of the Negroes but against the colossal prejudices of the white workers and makes no concession to them whatever."

At the time of the Trotsky-Swabeck discussion, the United States was in the grip of the severest depression it had ever had, with unemployment that year estimated between 13 and 17 million; as always, the unemployment rate was highest among black workers. Negroes were 12 million out of a total population of 122 million, according to the 1930 census. Seventy-nine percent of the Negroes still lived in the South, and 57 percent lived in rural areas. (By the mid-1960s migration had reduced the proportion of Negroes in the South to around one-half, and the proportion in rural areas to around one-fourth.) In the recent 1932 national election, the combined vote of the Socialist Party and the Communist Party candidates for president was almost one million, which they have never equalled since. Franklin D. Roosevelt had been elected president on the Democratic ticket, with a Southern segregationist as his vice-president, but had not yet taken office. The big switchover of Negro votes to the Democratic Party came later, starting in 1934. There was one lone Negro in

Congress, a Republican from Chicago. Union membership was pitifully small—between 2 and 3 million—and restricted mainly to craft unionists, among whom Negroes were few and far between. The CIO, the unionization of the mass industries, and the beginning of a Negro toehold in the labor movement were still the music of the future. The only area of common action between white and black workers was in the unemployed movements, whose membership was small. There were eight lynchings recorded in 1932, twenty-eight in 1933. The Garvey movement had collapsed, and hardly anyone had heard of the Nation of Islam (Black Muslims), which had been formed in Detroit in 1930. NAACP membership and influence, never great, had dwindled during the depression. There was no Congress of Racial Equality (CORE) or Student Non-violent Coordinating Committee (SNCC) or Southern Christian Leadership Conference (SCLC). No civil rights legislation had been passed since the preceding century, and the capitalist parties weren't even pretending that they would pass any. By and large, the black people were strictly on the defensive in 1933, struggling just to survive.

The Discussion
in Prinkipo

The Negro Question in America[1]

Prinkipo, Turkey
February 28, 1933

Swabeck:[2] We have in this question within the American League no noticeable differences of an important character, nor have we yet formulated a program. I present therefore only the views which we have developed in general.

How must we view the position of the American Negro: As a national minority or as a racial minority? This is of the greatest importance for our program.

The Stalinists maintain as their main slogan the one of

---

1. From the translation by Arne Swabeck in the *Internal Bulletin*, Communist League of America, no. 12, April 19, 1933. The Trotsky portions of this transcript have been retranslated from the German for this edition by Russell Block, by permission of the Harvard College Library.

2. Arne Swabeck (1890-   ), who was born in Denmark, was a founder of the American CP and the CLA. National secretary of the CLA in the early 1930s, he was its delegate to an international conference of the Left Opposition held in Paris in February 1933. From there he visited Trotsky in Turkey to have discussions about American problems. He became a Maoist in the late fifties and left the SWP in 1967.

self-determination for the Negroes and demand in connection therewith a separate state and state rights for the Negroes in the Black Belt. The practical application of the latter demand has revealed much opportunism. On the other hand, I acknowledge that in the practical work amongst the Negroes, despite the numerous mistakes, the [Communist] party can also record some achievements. For example in the Southern textile strikes, where to a large extent the color lines were broken down.

Weisbord,[3] I understand, is in agreement with the slogan of self-determination and separate state rights. He maintains that is the application of the theory of the permanent revolution for America.[4]

We proceed from the actual situation: There are approximately thirteen million Negroes in America; the majority are in the Southern states (Black Belt). In the Northern states the Negroes are concentrated in the industrial communities as industrial workers; in the South they are mainly farmers and sharecroppers.

Trotsky: Do they rent from the state or from private owners?

Swabeck: From private owners, from white farmers and plantation owners; some Negroes own the land they till.

The Negro population of the North is kept on a lower

---

3. Albert Weisbord (1900-1977), formerly a union organizer in the American CP, was the leader of a small group called the Communist League of Struggle that existed 1931-37. In 1933 the CLS claimed to be in agreement with the policies of the International Left Opposition, but it never joined because there were too many political differences. Weisbord supported the U.S. government in World War II.

4. Trotsky's theory of permanent revolution is expounded in his book *The Permanent Revolution* (Pathfinder, 1974). In general, this theory rejects the Social Democratic and Stalinist concept that in the era of imperialism the revolutionary process in the underdeveloped countries must take place in "stages" (first a stage of capitalist development, to be followed at some time in the future by a socialist transformation), and contends that the process will be continuous, or "permanent," passing swiftly to a postcapitalist stage. Specifically, the theory emphasizes the revolutionary potential and dynamic of the most exploited classes and strata and the most oppressed nations and nationalities.

level—economically, socially, and culturally; in the South, under oppressive Jim Crow conditions. They are barred from many important trade unions. During and since the war the migration from the South has increased; perhaps about four to five million Negroes now live in the North. The Northern Negro population is overwhelmingly proletarian, but also in the South the proletarianization is progressing.

Today none of the Southern states has a Negro majority. This lends emphasis to the heavy migration to the North. We put the question thus: Are the Negroes, in a political sense, a national minority or a racial minority? The Negroes have become fully assimilated, Americanized, and their life in America has overbalanced the traditions of the past, modified and changed them. We cannot consider the Negroes a national minority in the sense of having their own separate language. They have no special national customs, or special national culture or religion; nor have they any special national minority interests. It is impossible to speak of them as a national minority in this sense. It is therefore our opinion that the American Negroes are a racial minority whose position and interests are subordinated to the class relations of the country and depending upon them.

To us the Negroes represent an important factor in the class struggle, almost a decisive factor. They are an important section of the proletariat. There is also a Negro petty bourgeoisie in America, but not as powerful or as influential or playing the role of the petty bourgeoisie and bourgeoisie among the nationally oppressed peoples (colonial).

The Stalinist slogan "self-determination" is in the main based upon an estimate of the American Negroes as a national minority, to be won over as allies. To us the question occurs: Do we want to win the Negroes as allies on such a basis, and who do we want to win, the Negro proletariat or the Negro petty bourgeoisie? To us it appears that we will with this slogan win mainly the petty bourgeoisie, and we cannot have much interest in winning them as allies on such a basis. We recognize that the poor farmers and sharecroppers are the closest allies of the proletariat, but it is our opinion that they can be won as such mainly on the basis of the class struggle. Compromise on this principled question would put the petty-bourgeois allies ahead of the proletariat and the poor farmers as well. We recognize the existence of definite stages of development, which require specific slogans. But the Stalinist slogan appears to us to lead directly to the "democratic dictatorship of the proletariat and peasantry."[5] The unity of the workers, black and white, we must prepare proceeding from a class basis, but in that it is necessary to also recognize the racial issues and in addition to the class slogans also advance the racial slogans. It is our opinion that in this respect the main slogan should be "social, political, and economic equality for the Negroes," as well as the slogans which flow therefrom. This slogan is naturally quite different from the Stalinist slogan of self-determination for a national minority. The [Communist] party leaders maintain that the Negro workers and farmers can be won only on the basis of this slogan. To begin with it was advanced for the Negroes throughout the country, but today only for the Southern states. It is our opinion that we can win the Negro workers only on a class basis, advancing also the racial slogans for the necessary intermediary stages of development. In this manner we believe also the poor Negro farmers can best be won as direct allies.

In the main the problem of slogans in regard to the Negro question is the problem of a practical program. How will the Negroes be won over? We believe primarily with racial slogans: Equality with whites and the slogans which flow from this.

Trotsky: The point of view of the American comrades

---

5. The Stalinists used this term in the 1920s and 1930s to justify their support for certain bourgeois forces, especially in the Far East. They claimed that a victory for Chiang Kai-shek in the second Chinese revolution, 1925-27, would result in a "democratic dictatorship of the proletariat and peasantry." Chiang's victory actually resulted in a counterrevolutionary bourgeois-military dictatorship that suppressed the workers and peasants until it was overthrown in 1949.

appears to me not fully convincing. The right of self-determination is a democratic demand. Our American comrades counterpose the liberal demand to this democratic demand. This liberal demand is, moreover, complicated. I understand what political equality means. But what is the meaning of economic and social equality within capitalist society? Does that mean a demand to public opinion that all should enjoy the equal protection of the laws? But that is political equality. The slogan "political, economic, and social equality" sounds ambiguous and is thus false.

The Negroes are a race and not a nation. Nations grow out of racial material under definite conditions. The Negroes in Africa are not yet a nation but they are in the process of forming a nation. The American Negroes are on a higher cultural level. But since they are under the pressure of the Americans they become interested in the development of the Negroes in Africa. The American Negro will develop leaders for Africa, that one can say with certainty, and that in turn will influence the development of political consciousness in America.

We of course do not obligate the Negroes to become a nation; whether they are is a question of their consciousness, that is, what they desire and what they strive for. We say: If the Negroes want that then we must fight against imperialism to the last drop of blood, so that they gain the right, wherever and however they please, to separate a piece of land for themselves. The fact that they are today not a majority in any state does not matter. It is not a question of the authority of the states but of the Negroes. That there are and will be whites in areas that are overwhelmingly Negro is not the question, and we do not need to break our heads over the possibility that sometime the whites will be suppressed by the Negroes. In any case the suppression of the Negroes pushes them toward a political and national unity.

That the slogan "self-determination" will win over the petty bourgeois more than the workers—that argument holds good also for the slogan of equality. It is clear that those Negro elements who play more of a public role (businessmen, intellectuals, lawyers, etc.) are more active and react more actively against inequality. It is possible to say that the liberal demand as well as the democratic one in the first instance will attract the petty bourgeois and only later the workers.

If the situation was such that in America common actions took place involving white and black workers, that class fraternization already was a fact, then perhaps our comrades' arguments would have a basis (I do not say that it would be correct); then perhaps we would divide the black workers from the white if we began to raise the slogan "self-determination."

But today the white workers in relation to the Negroes are the oppressors, scoundrels, who persecute the black and the yellow, hold them in contempt, and lynch them. If the Negro workers unite with their own petty bourgeois, that is because they are not yet sufficiently developed to defend their elementary rights. To the workers in the Southern states the liberal demand for equal rights would undoubtedly mean progress, but the demand for self-determination, even greater progress. However, with the slogan "equal rights" they can be misled more easily ("according to the law you have this equality").

When we are so far that the Negroes say "we want autonomy," they then take a position hostile toward American imperialism. At that stage the workers will already be much more determined than the petty bourgeoisie. The workers will then see that the petty bourgeoisie is incapable of struggle and gets nowhere, but they will also recognize simultaneously that the white Communist workers fight for their demands and that will push them, the Negro proletarians, toward communism.

Weisbord is correct in a certain sense that the self-determination of the Negroes belongs to the question of the permanent revolution in America. The Negroes will, through their awakening, through their demand for autonomy, and through the democratic mobilization of their forces, be pushed on toward a class basis. The petty bourgeoisie will take up the demand for equal rights and for self-determination but will prove absolutely incapable

in the struggle; the Negro proletariat will march over the
petty bourgeoisie in the direction toward the proletarian
revolution. That is perhaps for them the most important
road. I can therefore see no reason why we should not
advance the demand for self-determination.

I am not sure if the Negroes in the South do not speak
their own Negro language. Now, at a time when they are
being lynched just because of being Negroes they naturally
fear to speak their Negro language; but when they are set
free their Negro language will come alive again. I would
advise the American comrades to study this question very
seriously, including the language in the Southern states.
For all these reasons I would in this question rather lean
toward the standpoint of the [Communist] party; of course,
with the observation that I have never studied this question and that I proceed here from general considerations. I
base myself only upon the arguments brought forward by
the American comrades. I find them insufficient and
consider them a certain concession to the point of view of
American chauvinism, which seems to me to be dangerous.

What can we lose in this question when we go further
with our demands than the Negroes themselves do at
present? We do not compel them to separate from the state,
but they have the full right to self-determination when
they so desire and we will support and defend them with
all the means at our disposal in the winning of this right,
the same as we defend all oppressed peoples.

Swabeck: I admit that you have advanced powerful
arguments, but I am not yet entirely convinced. The
existence of a special Negro language in the Southern
states is possible, but in general all American Negroes
speak English. They are fully assimilated. Their religion is
the American Baptist and the language in their churches
is likewise English.

Economic equality we do not at all understand in the
sense of the law. In the North (as of course also in the
Southern states), the wages for Negroes are always lower
than for white workers and mostly their hours are longer;
that is, so to say, accepted as natural. In addition the
Negroes are allotted the most disagreeable work. It is

because of these conditions that we demand economic equality for the Negro workers.

We do not contest the right of the Negroes to self-determination. That is not the issue of our disagreement with the Stalinists. But we contest the correctness of the slogan of self-determination as a means to win the Negro masses. The impulse of the Negro population is first of all in the direction toward equality in a social, political, and economic sense. At present the party advances the slogan for self-determination only for the Southern states. Of course, one can hardly expect that the Negroes from the Northern industries should want to return to the South, and there are no indications of such a desire. On the contrary. Their unformulated demand is for social, political, and economic equality based upon the conditions under which they live. That is also the case in the South. It is because of this that we believe this to be the important racial slogan. We do not look upon the Negroes as being under national oppression in the same sense as the oppressed colonial peoples. It is our opinion that the slogan of the Stalinists tends to lead the Negroes away from the class basis and more in the direction of the racial basis. That is the main reason for our being opposed to it. We are of the belief that the racial slogan in the sense as presented by us leads directly toward the class basis.

Frank:[6] Are there in America special Negro movements?

Swabeck: Yes, several. First we had the Garvey movement, based upon the aim of migration to Africa.[7] It had a large following but busted up as a swindle. Now there is not much left of it. Its slogan was the creation of a Negro

----

6. Pierre Frank (1905-   ), a founder of the French Left Opposition, was a secretary of Trotsky in Turkey, 1932-33. Since the end of World War II, he has been a member of the International Secretariat of the Fourth International and its successor, the United Secretariat.

7. The Universal Negro Improvement Association was organized by Marcus Garvey (1887-1940) in his native Jamaica in 1914 and in the United States in 1916. It became an international "Back to Africa" movement, with a following of hundreds of thousands in the U.S. at its height, between World War I and the mid-twenties.

republic in Africa. Other Negro movements in the main rest upon a foundation of social and political equality demands as, for example, the League [National Association] for the Advancement of Colored People.[8] This is a large racial movement.

Trotsky: I also believe that the demand for equal rights should remain, and I do not speak *against* this demand. It is progressive to the extent that it has not yet been realized. Comrade Swabeck's explanation in regard to the question of economic equality is very important. But that alone does not decide the question of the Negroes' fate as such, the question of the nation, etc. According to the arguments of the American comrades, one could say for example that Belgium too has no rights as a nation. The Belgians are Catholics and a large section of them speak French. What if France wanted to annex them with such an argument? Also the Swiss people, through their historical connections, feel themselves to be one nation despite different languages and religions. An abstract criterion is not decisive in this question; far more decisive is the historical consciousness of a group, their feelings, their impulses. But that too is not determined accidentally but rather by the situation and all the attendant circumstances. The question of religion has absolutely nothing to do with this question of nationhood. The Baptism of the Negro is something entirely different from Rockefeller's Baptism.[9] These are two different religions.

The political argument rejecting the demand for self-determination is doctrinairism. That is what we always heard in Russia in regard to the question of self-determination. The Russian experience has shown us that the groups which live a peasant existence retain peculiarities—their customs, their language, etc.—and given the opportunity these characteristics develop.

The Negroes have not yet awakened, and they are not

---

8. The National Association for the Advancement of Colored People (NAACP) was organized in 1909 by liberals, Social Democrats, and civil libertarians, including W. E. B. Du Bois.

9. This refers to the oil baron John D. Rockefeller (1839-1937) or his son, John D. Rockefeller, Jr. (1874-1960).

yet united with the white workers. Ninety-nine point nine percent of the American workers are chauvinists; in relation to the Negroes they are hangmen as they are also toward the Chinese, etc. It is necessary to make them understand that the American state is not their state and that they do not have to be the guardians of this state. Those American workers who say: "The Negroes should separate if they so desire, and we will defend them against our American police"—those are revolutionists, I have confidence in them.

The argument that the slogan for self-determination leads away from the class point of view is an adaptation to the ideology of the white workers. The Negro can be developed to a class point of view only when the white worker is educated. On the whole the question of the colonial people is in the first instance a question of the education of the metropolitan worker.

The American worker is indescribably reactionary. This can be seen now in the fact that he has not yet even been won to the idea of social insurance. Because of this the American Communists are obligated to advance reform demands.

If the Negroes do not at present demand self-determination it is of course for the same reason that the white workers do not yet advance the slogan of the dictatorship of the proletariat.[10] The Negroes have not yet got it into their heads that they dare to carve out a piece of the great and mighty States for themselves. But the white workers must meet the Negroes halfway and say to them: "If you want to separate you will have our support." The Czech workers as well came to Communism only through disillusionment with their own state.

I believe that because of the unprecedented political and theoretical backwardness and the unprecedented economic progressiveness in America, the awakening of the working class will proceed quite rapidly. The old ideological cover-

---

10. This is the Marxist term for the form of rule by the working class that follows rule by the capitalist class (dictatorship of the bourgeoisie). Modern equivalents for the term are "workers' state" and "workers' democracy."

ing will burst, all questions will emerge at once, and since the country is so economically mature the adaptation of the political and theoretical to the economic level will be achieved very rapidly. It is then possible that the Negroes will become the most advanced section. We have already a similar example in Russia. The Russians were the European Negroes. It is very possible that the Negroes will proceed through self-determination to the proletarian dictatorship in a couple of gigantic strides, ahead of the great bloc of white workers. They will then be the vanguard. I am absolutely sure that they will in any case fight better than the white workers. That, however, can happen only provided the Communist Party carries on an uncompromising, merciless struggle not against the supposed national prepossessions of the Negroes but against the colossal prejudices of the white workers and makes no concession to them whatever.

Swabeck: It is then your opinion that the slogan for self-determination will be a means to set the Negroes into motion against American imperialism?

Trotsky: Naturally, by carving their own state out of mighty America, and doing that with the support of the white workers, the Negroes' self-confidence will develop enormously.

The reformists and the revisionists have written a great deal to the effect that capitalism is carrying on the work of civilization in Africa, and if the peoples of Africa are left to themselves they will be all the more exploited by businessmen, etc., much more than now where they at least have a certain measure of legal protection.

To a certain extent this argument can be correct. But in this case also it is foremost a question of the European workers: Without their liberation real colonial liberation is not possible. If the white worker performs the role of the oppressor he cannot liberate himself, much less the colonial peoples. The right of self-determination of the colonial peoples can in certain periods lead to different results; in the final instance, however, it will lead to the struggle against imperialism and to the liberation of the colonial peoples.

Before the war [World War I] the Austrian Social Democracy (particularly Renner)[11] also posed the question of the national minorities abstractly. They argued likewise that the slogan for self-determination would only lead the workers away from a class point of view, and that economically the minority state could not exist independently. Was this way of putting the question correct or false? It was abstract. The Austrian Social Democrats said that the national minorities were not nations. What do we see today? The separated pieces [of the old Austro-Hungarian empire] exist—bad to be sure, but they exist. In Russia the Bolsheviks always fought for the self-determination of the national minorities, including the right of complete separation. And yet, after having achieved self-determination these groups remained with the Soviet Union. If the Austrian Social Democracy had carried out a correct policy regarding this question earlier, they would have said to the national minority groups: "You have the full right to self-determination, we have no interest whatever in keeping you in the hands of the Habsburg[12] monarchy"—it would then have been possible after the revolution to create a great Danube federation. The dialectic of development shows that where tight centralism existed, the state went to pieces, and where complete self-determination was enacted, a real state emerged and remained united.

The Negro question is of enormous importance for America. The League must undertake a serious discussion of this question, perhaps in an internal bulletin.

---

11. Karl Renner (1870-1950) was the Social Democratic chancellor of Austria, 1919-20, and president of its national assembly, 1931-33.

12. The Habsburgs were a family of German princes that furnished the rulers of Austria from the thirteenth century until they were overthrown by the revolution of 1918, which brought an end to World War I.

C. L. R. James, 1938

Charles Curtiss, 1938

The Discussions
in Coyoacán

Editorial Introduction

The "serious discussion" recommended by Trotsky in 1933 was not held until several years later. One month before the Trotsky-Swabeck exchange, Adolf Hitler had been appointed chancellor of Germany. Fascism came to power without the large German Communist Party firing a single shot in resistance. To Trotsky and the Left Opposition, this signified the definitive bankruptcy of the Communist International as a revolutionary organization. So they abandoned the perspective of reforming the Communist parties and proclaimed, in 1933, the need to build a new Marxist international and revolutionary parties all over the world.

The Communist League of America ceased to consider itself a faction of the CP and turned in other directions to gather the forces for a new party in the United States. At the end of 1934 it merged with the American Workers Party, headed by A. J. Muste, to form the Workers Party. In 1936 the members of the Workers Party entered the Socialist Party in order to merge with its revolutionary left wing. In 1937 the Socialist Party expelled this left wing, which constituted itself, at the start of 1938, as the Socialist Workers Party. Trotsky and the International

33

Left Opposition also sought out other leftward-moving forces with the result that in September 1938 the Fourth International, World Party of Socialist Revolution, was able to hold its founding conference in France. The SWP was an affiliate of the Fourth International until the end of 1940, when the passage of reactionary legislation in Washington compelled it to sever formal ties with the new International, although it remained in political solidarity with it.

After deciding that a new party was necessary in 1933, the CLA and its successors turned toward work in the mass movements, particularly the unions and unemployed organizations. As a result, they recruited workers, black as well as white, and began to get a different and closer grasp of the so-called Negro question. The SWP's practical activities among black workers stimulated a demand for greater attention to the Negro struggle in the party's program and literature and for theoretical clarification on the nature and direction of the Negro struggle. The "serious discussion" at last took place at the second convention of the SWP, held in July 1939.

But Trotsky's advice and suggestions again were sought, this time in a series of three discussions held at his home in Coyoacán, Mexico, where he had received asylum in 1937. The principal figure in the delegation that visited him was C. L. R. James, a revolutionary black intellectual from the West Indies and a leader of the Fourth International in Britain. James had been living in the United States for the previous six months, acquainting himself with, among other things, the state of the American Negro community.

As a basis for the discussions, James prepared some preliminary notes. On the self-determination question, he wrote:

> The Negro must be won for socialism. There is no other way out for him in America or elsewhere. But he must be won on the basis of his own experience and his own activity. There is no other way for him to learn, nor for that matter, for any other group of toilers! *If he wanted self-determination,* then however reactionary it might be in

every other respect, it would be the business of the revolutionary party to raise that slogan. If after the revolution he insisted on carrying out that slogan and forming his own Negro state, the revolutionary party would have to stand by its promises and (similarly to its treatment of large masses of the peasantry) patiently trust to economic development and education to achieve an integration. But the Negro, fortunately for socialism, does not want self-determination [*Internal Bulletin,* Socialist Workers Party, no. 9, June 1939].

Because Negroes "individually and in the mass . . . remain profoundly suspicious of whites," James proposed, as an alternative to any self-determination proposals, the formation of an all-black movement that would fight for equality in all areas—social, economic, and political. This the Negro masses would respond to, and this would set them "in motion, the only way in which they will learn the realities of political activity and be brought to realize the necessity of mortal struggle against capitalism." The proposed Negro organization would not be an SWP "front"—it would be open to all black militants, SWP members among others. James also included proposals for organizing the SWP's work in the Negro community through a special party department, and other measures of a practical character.

The first discussion, held April 4, dealt with the question of self-determination. The other two, on April 5 and April 11, were concerned mainly with the proposed Negro organization.

The 1940 census, a year later, showed there were thirteen million Negroes in the country, 74 percent in the South and 52 percent in rural areas; the biggest migrations out of the South and to urban areas were not to begin until World War II, which was just around the corner. Not as bad as in 1933, unemployment was still very high and remained that way until the war began. The number of lynchings recorded in 1938 was six, and in 1939 it was three. Most Negroes who were able to vote voted Democratic, not because the Democrats offered anything on civil rights but because Roosevelt's New Deal promised economic reform and welfare concessions. There was still only one Negro in Congress, this time a Chicago Democrat. The National Negro Congress, formed in 1936 by Stalinists, liberals, and Social Democrats, claimed to represent more than five hundred organizations and sought to become the chief organization speaking for the Negro community. But it made little headway in the ghetto and by 1940 it was split, partly because of differences over the war, and it became a Stalinist front, with declining influence. The Communist Party recruited thousands of black members during the 1930s, but it lost most of them when the Soviet Union sold oil to Italy during the Italian invasion of Ethiopia in 1935 and when the CP became an apologist for the Democrats during Roosevelt's second term. A few black nationalist and separatist groups were formed during the 1930s, but they made little headway. Many black militants thought that the most promising development of the decade was the explosion of labor radicalism, the formation of the CIO and the unionization of the mass industries, as a result of which Negro workers, welcomed into a part of the labor movement for the first time, joined by the hundreds of thousands; and some of the most radical Negroes believed, at least until the 1950s, that Negro progress could best be guaranteed through collaboration with the CIO.

In the first of the three discussions Trotsky rejected all arguments against supporting the right of Negroes to self-determination (along with a few poor arguments in favor of it). Better acquainted with the CP's position, he now considered its "attitude of making an imperative slogan of it" to be false and tactless. "I do not propose for the party to advocate, I do not propose to inject, but only to proclaim our obligation to support the struggle for self-determination if the Negroes themselves want it. It is not a question of our Negro comrades. It is a question of thirteen or fourteen million Negroes. The majority of them are very backward. They are not very clear as to what they wish now, and we must give them a credit for the future. They will decide then."

Repeatedly he expressed the idea that "we must not base ourselves on the status quo": The fact that the Negroes were not demanding self-determination now did not mean that they might not demand it later. He mentioned some of the conditions under which the demand might arise—if there was a Japanese invasion of the U.S.; if fascism came to power in the U.S.; and at the beginning of a working class revolution. Of the latter he said, "They will enter with a great distrust of the whites. We must remain neutral in the matter and hold the door open for both possibilities and promise our full support if they wish to create their own independent state."

It did not surprise Trotsky that now, while "the whites are so powerful, so cruel, and so rich . . . the poor Negro sharecropper does not say, even to himself, that he will take a part of this country for himself." But what would happen when the Negroes got a breathing spell, became better organized, acquired greater political experience and unity—would they dare to say it then? The realization of the self-determination slogan, Trotsky stressed, "can be reached only as the thirteen or fourteen million Negroes feel that the domination by the whites is terminated" or in the process of being terminated—that is, when the Negroes feel they have a better chance of winning, when they have acquired powerful allies, when the white oppressors are losing some of their previous advantages and the relationship of forces is changing.

The idea that the consequences of self-determination might be "reactionary" Trotsky dismissed as abstract and wrong: "To fight for the possibility of realizing an independent state is a sign of great moral and political awakening. It would be a tremendous revolutionary step." Hence there was nothing grudging or hesitant about the way he endorsed the right of self-determination.

In the second discussion, Trotsky became convinced that it would be correct to experiment with the formation of an all-black action organization. The main thing he emphasized was that the organization should be oriented to the masses and not to the intellectuals, who "keep themselves separated from the masses, always with the desire to take on the Anglo-Saxon culture and of becoming an integral part of Anglo-Saxon life."

The third discussion was about plans for the proposed Negro organization, but Trotsky devoted the major part of his remarks to what he considered "the first question," the SWP's attitude to the Negro struggle. He found it "a very disquieting symptom" that the SWP had done so little, and warned that the party "cannot develop—it will degenerate" unless it entered the struggle in a serious fashion. The Negroes are "the most dynamic milieu of the working class," the group most capable of revolutionary courage and sacrifice, whose conscious elements are destined to become "a vanguard of the working class." If the SWP could not find its way to them, "then we are not worthy at all. The permanent revolution and all the rest would be only a lie."

Self-Determination
for the American Negroes[13]

Coyoacán, Mexico
April 4, 1939

Trotsky: Comrade James[14] proposes that we discuss the Negro question in three parts, the first to be devoted to the programmatic question of self-determination for the Negroes.

[Some statistical material was introduced which was not included in the report.]

---

13. This and the following two transcripts are reprinted from the *Internal Bulletin,* Socialist Workers Party, no. 9, June 1939. For security reasons, pseudonyms were used in that version of the transcript ("Crux" for Trotsky, "J. R. Johnson" for C. L. R. James, "Carlos" for Charles Curtiss, etc.); wherever possible, such pseudonyms are replaced by the real names here. A stenographer's note explained that the transcripts were "rough notes uncorrected by the participants."

14. C. L. R. James (1901-   ), who was born in Trinidad, joined the Fourth Internationalist movement in Britain in 1935. He was a delegate

James: The basic proposals for the Negro question have already been distributed, and here it is only necessary to deal with the question of self-determination. No one denies the Negroes' right to self-determination. It is a question of whether we should advocate it. In Africa and in the West Indies we advocate self-determination because a large majority of the people want it. In Africa the great masses of the people look upon self-determination as a restoration of their independence. In the West Indies, where we have a population similar in origin to the Negroes in America, there has been developing a national sentiment. The Negroes are a majority. Already we hear ideas, among the more advanced, of a West Indian nation, and it is highly probable that, even let us suppose that the Negroes were offered full and free rights as citizens of the British Empire, they would probably oppose it and wish to be absolutely free and independent. Therefore, both in Africa and in the West Indies, the International African Service Bureau[15] advocates self-determination. It is progressive. It is a step in the right direction. We weaken the enemy. It puts the workers in a position to make great progress toward socialism.

In America the situation is different. The Negro desperately wants to be an American citizen. He says, "I have been here from the beginning; I did all the work here in the early days. Jews, Poles, Italians, Swedes, and others come

---

to its international conferences in 1936 and 1938; at the latter he was elected to the International Executive Committee of the Fourth International. By this time he had already written *The Black Jacobins* and *World Revolution*. At the end of 1938 he moved to the United States, where he became part of the SWP leadership. He quit the SWP during a split in 1940, returned in 1947, and left again for good in 1951.

15. The International African Service Bureau was a small radical organization in Britain that sought to organize support and solidarity with colonial independence and labor struggles. Its leaders included C. L. R. James and George Padmore (1903-1959), another West Indian, a former Comintern functionary, and a member of the Independent Labour Party; he later became adviser to Kwame Nkrumah of Ghana. The bureau's journal was *International African Opinion*. James wanted, among other things, to develop support in the U.S. for the bureau and its journal.

here and have all the privileges. You say that some of the Germans are spies. I will never spy. I have nobody for whom to spy. And yet you exclude me from the army and from the rights of citizenship."

In Poland and Catalonia there is a tradition of language, literature, and history to add to the economic and political oppression and to help weld the population in its progressive demand for self-determination. In America it is not so. Let us look at certain historic events in the development of the Negro in America.

Garvey raised the slogan "Back to Africa," but the Negroes who followed him did not believe for the most part that they were really going back to Africa. We know that those in the West Indies who were following him had not the slightest intention of going back to Africa, but they were glad to follow a militant leadership. And there is the case of the black woman who was pushed by a white woman in a street car and said to her, "You wait until Marcus gets into power and all you people will be treated in the way you deserve." Obviously she was not thinking of Africa.

There was however this concentration on the Negroes' problems simply because the white workers in 1919 were not developed. There was no political organization of any power calling upon the blacks and the whites to unite. The Negroes were just back from the war—militant and having no offer of assistance, they naturally concentrated on their own particular affairs.

In addition, however, we should note that in Chicago, where a race riot took place, the riot was deliberately provoked by the employers. Some time before it actually broke out, the black and white meatpackers had struck and had paraded through the Negro quarter in Chicago with the black population cheering the whites in the same way that they cheered the blacks. For the capitalists this was a very dangerous thing and they set themselves to creating race friction. At one stage, motor cars with white people in them sped through the Negro quarter shooting at all whom they saw. The capitalist press played up the differences and thus set the stage and initiated the riots that took place for dividing the population and driving the Negro back upon himself.

During the period of the crisis there was a rebirth of these nationalist movements. There was a movement toward the forty-ninth state,[16] and the movement concentrated around Liberia was developing. These movements assumed fairly large proportions up to at least 1934.

Then in 1936 came the organization of the CIO. John L. Lewis appointed a special Negro department.[17] The New Deal made gestures to the Negroes. Blacks and whites fought together in various struggles. These nationalist movements have tended to disappear as the Negro saw the opportunity to fight with the organized workers and to gain something.

The danger of our advocating and injecting a policy of self-determination is that it is the surest way to divide and confuse the workers in the South. The white workers have centuries of prejudice to overcome, but at the present time many of them are working with the Negroes in the Southern sharecroppers' union, and with the rise of the struggle there is every possibility that they will be able to overcome their agelong prejudices. But for us to propose that the Negro have this black state for himself is asking too much from the white workers, especially when the Negro himself is not making the same demand. The slogans of abolition of debts, confiscation of large proper-

---

16. The National Movement for the Establishment of the Forty-Ninth State was started in Chicago in the mid-1930s by Oscar C. Brown, a lawyer and businessman. It advocated self-determination through establishment of a Negro state as part of the Union, "an interdependent Commonwealth like any other of the present forty-eight states." It received little support and did not last long.

17. The CIO began as a faction, the Committee for Industrial Organization, inside the America Federation of Labor (AFL) in 1935. It became the Congress of Industrial Organizations in 1938 when its affiliated unions were expelled from the AFL for daring to organize the mass production industries on the basis of industrial unionism. The CIO attracted strong black support because, unlike most AFL unions, it welcomed the workers of all races in the industries it was trying to unionize. John L. Lewis (1880-1969) was president of the United Mine Workers and the principal leader of the CIO until his resignation in 1940. The AFL and CIO merged in 1955.

ties, etc., are quite sufficient to lead them both to fight together and on the basis of economic struggle to make a united fight for the abolition of social discrimination.

I therefore propose concretely: (1) That we are for the right of self-determination. (2) If some demand should arise among the Negroes for the right of self-determination we should support it. (3) We do not go out of our way to raise this slogan and place an unnecessary barrier between ourselves and socialism. (4) An investigation should be made into these movements—the one led by Garvey, the movement for the forty-ninth state, the movement centering around Liberia. Find out what groups of the population supported them and on this basis come to some opinion as to how far there is any demand among the Negroes for self-determination.

Curtiss:[18] It seems to me that the problem can be divided into a number of different phases:

On the question of self-determination, I think it is clear that while we are for self-determination, even to the point of independence, it does not necessarily mean that we favor independence. What we are in favor of is that in a certain case, in a certain locality, they have the right to decide for themselves whether or not they should be independent or what particular governmental arrangements they should have with the majority of the country.

On the question of self-determination being necessarily reactionary—I believe that is a little far-fetched. Self-determination for various nations and groups is not opposed to a future socialist world. I think the question was handled in a polemic between Lenin and Pyatakov[19] from the point of view of Russia—of self-determination for the various peoples of Russia while still building a united

18. Charles Curtiss (1908-   ) was a member of the SWP's National Committee. He was the Fourth International's representative in Mexico, 1938-39. He left the SWP in 1951 and joined the Socialist Party.

19. V. I. Lenin (1870-1924) was the principal leader of the Bolshevik Party and the Russian revolution of 1917, and the founder of the Soviet Union and the Communist International. Yuri Pyatakov (1890-1937) was an outstanding leader of the Bolshevik Party, expelled in 1927 because he belonged to the Left Opposition, led by Trotsky. He recanted and was

country. There is not necessarily a contradiction between the two. The socialist society will not be built upon subjugated people, but from a free people. The reactionary or progressive character of self-determination is determined by whether or not it will advance the social revolution. That is the criterion.

As to the point which was made, that we should not advocate a thing if the masses do not want it, that is not correct. We do not advocate things just because the masses want them. The basic question of socialism would come under that category. In the United States only a small percentage of the people want socialism, but still we advocate it. They may want war, but we oppose it. The questions we have to solve are as follows: Will it help in the destruction of American imperialism? If such a movement arises, will the people want it as the situation develops?

I take it that these nationalist movements of which you speak were carried on for years, and the struggle was carried on by a handful of people in each case, but in the moment of social crisis the masses rallied to such movements. The same can possibly happen in connection with self-determination of the Negroes.

It seems to me that the so-called Black Belt is a superexploited section of the American economy. It has all the characteristics of a subjugated section of an empire. It has all the extreme poverty and political inequality. It has the same financial structure—Wall Street exploits the petty-bourgeois elements and in turn the poor workers. It represents simply a field for investment and a source of profits. It has the characteristics of part of a colonial empire. It is also essentially a regional matter, for the whites have also been forced to feel a reaction against finance capital.

It would also be interesting to study the possible future

---

readmitted in 1928 and became a top official in Soviet industry. He was framed up and executed after the second Moscow trial. Lenin's 1916 polemics against Pyatakov, who was opposed to the right of self-determination for schematic reasons, are printed in Lenin's *Collected Works*, vol. 23.

development of the Negro question. We saw that when the Negroes were brought to the South they stayed there for many decades. When the war came, many emigrated to the North and there formed a part of the proletariat. That tendency can no longer operate. Capitalism is no longer expanding as it was before. As a matter of fact, during the depression many of them went back to the farms. It is possible that instead of a tendency to emigrate, there will now be a tendency for the Negro to stay in the South.

And there are other factors: The question of the cotton picking machine, which means that the workers will be thrown out of work by the thousands.

To get back to the question of self-determination. There is the possibility that in the midst of the social crisis the manifestation of radicalism takes a double phase: Along with the struggle for economic and social equality, there may be found the demand for the control of their own state. Even in Russia, when the Bolsheviks came to power, the Polish people were not satisfied that this would mean the end of oppression for them. They demanded the right to control their own destiny in their own way. Such a development is possible in the South.

The other questions are important, but I do not think they are basic—that a nation must have its own language, culture, and tradition. To a certain extent they have been developing a culture of their own. In any public library can be found books—fiction, anthologies, etc.—expressing a new racial feeling.

Now from the point of view of the United States, the withdrawal of the Black Belt means the weakening of American imperialism by the withdrawal of a big field of investment. That is a blow in favor of the American working class.

It seems to me that self-determination is not opposed to the struggle for social and political and economic equality. In the North such a struggle is immediate and the need is acute. In the North the slogan for economic and political equality is an agitational slogan—an immediate question. From the practical angle, no one suggests that we raise the slogan of self-determination as an agitational one, but as a programmatic one which may become agitational in the future.

There is another factor which might be called the psychological one. If the Negroes think that this is an attempt to segregate them, then it would be best to withhold the slogan until they are convinced that this is not the case.

Trotsky: I do not quite understand whether Comrade James proposes to eliminate the slogan of self-determination for the Negroes from our program, or is it that we do not say that we are ready to do everything possible for the self-determination of the Negroes if they want it themselves? It is a question for the party as a whole, if we eliminate it or not. We are ready to help them if they want it. As a party we can remain absolutely neutral on this. We cannot say it will be reactionary. It is not reactionary. We cannot tell them to set up a state because that will weaken imperialism and so will be good for us, the white workers. That would be against internationalism itself. We cannot say to them, "Stay here, even at the price of economic progress." We can say, "It is for you to decide. If you wish to take a part of the country, it is all right, but we do not wish to make the decision for you."

I believe that the differences between the West Indies, Catalonia, Poland, and the situation of the Negroes in the States are not so decisive. Rosa Luxemburg[20] was against self-determination for Poland. She felt that it was reactionary and fantastic, as fantastic as demanding the right to fly. It shows that she did not possess the necessary historic imagination in this case. The landlords and representatives of the Polish ruling class were also opposed to self-determination, for their own reasons.

Comrade James used three verbs: "support," "advocate,"

20. Rosa Luxemburg (1871-1919) is one of the most respected figures in the history of the Marxist movement. She was imprisoned in Germany for opposing World War I, helped to found the German CP, and was murdered by government troops after the Spartacist uprising of 1919. Her views on self-determination are printed in *Rosa Luxemburg Speaks* (Pathfinder, 1970) and *The National Question* (Monthly Review Press, 1976).

and "inject" the idea of self-determination. I do not propose for the party to advocate, I do not propose to inject, but only to proclaim our obligation to support the struggle for self-determination if the Negroes themselves want it. It is not a question of our Negro comrades. It is a question of thirteen or fourteen million Negroes. The majority of them are very backward. They are not very clear as to what they wish now, and we must give them a credit for the future. They will decide then.

What you said about the Garvey movement is interesting—but it proves that we must be cautious and broad and not base ourselves upon the status quo. The black woman who said to the white woman, "Wait until Marcus is in power. We will know how to treat you then," was simply expressing her desire for her own state. The American Negroes gathered under the banner of the "Back to Africa" movement because it seemed a possible fulfillment of their wish for their own home. They did not want actually to go to Africa. It was the expression of a mystic desire for a home in which they would be free of the domination of the whites, in which they themselves could control their own fate. That also was a wish for self-determination. It was once expressed by some in a religious form, and now it takes the form of a dream of an independent state. Here in the United States the whites are so powerful, so cruel, and so rich that the poor Negro sharecropper does not say, even to himself, that he will take a part of this country for himself. Garvey spoke in glowing terms, that it was beautiful and that here all would be wonderful. Any psychoanalyst will say that the real content of this dream was to have their own home. It is not an argument in favor of injecting the idea. It is only an argument by which we can foresee the possibility of their giving their dream a more realistic form.

Under the condition that Japan invades the United States and the Negroes are called upon to fight—they may come to feel themselves threatened first from one side and then from the other, and finally awakened, may say, "We have nothing to do with either of you. We will have our own state."

But the black state could enter into a federation. If the American Negroes succeeded in creating their own state, I am sure that after a few years of the satisfaction and pride of independence, they would feel the need of entering into a federation. Even if Catalonia, which is a very industrialized and highly developed province, had realized its independence, it would have been just a step to federation.

The Jews in Germany and Austria wanted nothing more than to be the best German chauvinists. The most miserable of all was the Social Democrat Austerlitz,[21] the editor of the *Arbeiterzeitung*. But now, with the turn of events, Hitler does not permit them to be German chauvinists. Now many of them have become Zionists and are Palestinian nationalists and anti-German. I saw a disgusting picture recently of a Jewish actor, arriving in America, bending down to kiss the soil of the United States. Then they will get a few blows from the fascist fists in the United States, and they will go to kiss the soil of Palestine.

There is another alternative to the successful revolutionary one. It is possible that fascism will come to power with its racial delirium and oppression, and the reaction of the Negro will be toward racial independence. Fascism in the United States will be directed against the Jews and the Negroes, but against the Negroes particularly, and in a most terrible manner. A "privileged" condition will be created for the American white workers on the backs of the Negroes. The Negroes have done everything possible to become an integral part of the United States, in a psychological as well as a political sense. We must foresee that their reaction will show its power during the revolution. They will enter with a great distrust of the whites. We must remain neutral in the matter and hold the door open for both possibilities and promise our full support if they wish to create their own independent state.

So far as I am informed, it seems to me that the CP's attitude of making an imperative slogan of it was false. It was a case of the whites saying to the Negroes, "You must create a ghetto for yourselves." It is tactless and false and

---

21. Friedrich Austerlitz (1862-1931) was a leader of the Austrian Social Democracy.

can only serve to repulse the Negroes. Their only interpretation can be that the whites want to be separated from them. Our Negro comrades, of course, have the right to participate more intimately in such developments. Our Negro comrades can say, "The Fourth International says that if it is our wish to be independent, it will help us in every way possible, but that the choice is ours. However, I, as a Negro member of the Fourth, hold a view that we must remain in the same state as the whites," and so on. He can participate in the formation of the political and racial ideology of the Negroes.

James: I am very glad that we have had this discussion, because I agree with you entirely. It seems to be the idea in America that we should advocate it as the CP has done. You seem to think that there is a greater possibility of the Negroes wanting self-determination than I think is probable. But we have a 100 percent agreement on the idea which you have put forward that we should be neutral in the development.

Trotsky: It is the word "reactionary" that bothered me.

James: Let me quote from the document: "If he wanted self-determination, then however reactionary it might be in every other respect, it would be the business of the revolutionary party to raise that slogan." I consider the idea of separating as a step backward so far as a socialist society is concerned. If the white workers extend a hand to the Negro, he will not want self-determination.

Trotsky: It is too abstract, because the realization of this slogan can be reached only as the thirteen or fourteen million Negroes feel that the domination by the whites is terminated. To fight for the possibility of realizing an independent state is a sign of great moral and political awakening. It would be a tremendous revolutionary step. This ascendancy would immediately have the best economic consequences.

Curtiss: I think that an analogy could be made in connection with the collectives and the distribution of large estates. One might consider the breaking up of large estates into small plots as reactionary, but it is not necessarily so. But this question is up to the peasants, whether they want to operate the estates collectively or individually. We advise the peasants, but we do not force them—it is up to them. Some would say that the breaking up of the large estates into small plots would be economically reactionary, but that is not so.

Trotsky: This was also the position of Rosa Luxemburg. She maintained that self-determination would be as reactionary as the breaking up of the large estates.

Curtiss: The question of self-determination is also tied up with the question of land and must be looked upon not only in its political but also in its economic manifestations.

A Negro Organization

Coyoacán, Mexico
April 5, 1939

(Comrade James's manuscript read by the comrades prior to the meeting.)

Trotsky: It is very important whether it is advisable and whether it is possible to create such an organization on our own initiative. Our movement is familiar with such forms as the party, the trade union, the educational organization, the cooperative; but this is a new type of organization which does not coincide with the traditional forms. We must consider the question from all sides as to whether it is advisable or not and what the form of our participation in this organization should be.

If another party had organized such a mass movement, we would surely participate as a fraction, providing that it included workers, poor petty bourgeois, poor farmers, and so on. We would enter for the purpose of educating the best elements and winning them for our party. But this is another thing. What is proposed here is that we take the initiative. Even without knowing the concrete situation in

Negro circles in the United States, I believe we can admit that no one but our party is capable of forming such a movement on a realistic basis. Of course, the movements guided by the improvisatorial Negro leaders, as we saw them in the past, more or less expressed the unwillingness or the incapacity, the perfidy of all the existing parties. None of the parties can now assume such a task because they are either pro-Roosevelt[22] imperialists or anti-Roosevelt imperialists. Such an organization of the oppressed Negroes signifies to them the weakening of "democracy" and of big business. This is also true of the Stalinists. Thus, the only party capable of beginning such an action is our own party.

But the question remains as to whether we can take upon ourselves the initiative of forming such an organization of Negroes as Negroes—not for the purpose of winning some elements to our party but for the purpose of doing systematic educational work in order to elevate them politically. What should be the form—what the correct line of our party? That is our question.

Curtiss: As I have already said to Comrade James, the Communist Party organized the American Negro Labor Congress and the League of Struggle for Negro Rights.[23] Neither one had great success. Both were very poorly organized. I personally think that such an organization should be organized, but I think it should be done carefully and only after a study of all the factors involved and also of the causes of the breakdown of the two organizations mentioned. We must be sure of a mass base. To create a

---

22. Franklin D. Roosevelt (1882-1945) was Democratic president of the U.S., 1933-45. His New Deal reforms sought to overcome the Great Depression while containing the militancy of the workers. The Stalinists were his most uncritical supporters in the labor movement from 1935 until the Stalin-Hitler pact in 1939.

23. The American Negro Labor Congress (ANLC) was created in 1925 and lasted until 1930, when, at a conference in St. Louis, its name was changed to the League of Struggle for Negro Rights (LSNR). The ANLC emphasized the fight for equality; the LSNR supported the right of self-determination in the Black Belt. The CP dissolved the LSNR in 1936, when the National Negro Congress was formed.

shadow of ourselves would serve only to discredit the idea and would benefit no one.

Trotsky: Who were the leaders of these organizations?

Curtiss: Fort-Whiteman, Owen, Haywood, Ford, Patterson; Bob Minor was the leader of the CP's Negro work. [24]

Trotsky: Who are the leaders now?

Curtiss: Most of them are in the CP, so far as I know. Some have dropped out of the movement.

Owen: Comrade James seems to have the idea that there is a good chance of building such an organization in the immediate future. I would like to have him elaborate.

James: I think that it should be a success because on my arrival in New York I met great numbers of Negroes and spoke to many Negro organizations. I brought forward the point of view of the Fourth International, particularly on the war question, and in every case there was great applause and a very enthusiastic reception of the ideas. Great numbers of these Negroes hated the Communist Party, agreed entirely with the program put forward by the International African Service Bureau, and were extremely interested in the journal *International African Opinion*. Up to the last convention, 79 percent of the Negro membership of the CP in New York State, 1,579 people, had left the CP. I met many of the representative ones, and they were now willing to form a Negro organization but did not wish to join the Fourth International. I had come to the conclusion that there was this possibility of a Negro organization before I left New York, but waited until I had gone through various towns in the States and got into contact with the Negro population there. And I found that

---

24. Lovett Fort-Whiteman was an early CP member and national organizer of the ANLC. Harry Haywood (1898-   ) was the first national secretary of the LSNR and one of the strongest advocates of the CP's "self-determination" line; he broke with the CP when it finally withdrew all support for self-determination in 1959. James W. Ford (1893-1957) was the CP vice-presidential candidate in 1932, 1936, and 1940. William Patterson (1891-   ) was a leading CP member who was the executive secretary for the International Labor Defense and the Civil Rights Congress. Robert Minor (1884-1952) was a cartoonist who became a CP leader.

the impressions that I had gathered in New York corresponded to those that I found on the tour.

In Boston, for instance, I went to a Barbados organization and there found about twenty or thirty people who had some sort of free society, but after having spoken to them for five or ten minutes they became very much interested in the political questions that I raised; and the chairman told me that if I wanted to come back to Boston he could arrange a Negro meeting for me at which we would have about seven hundred people. I do not think that it is too much to say that that was characteristic of the general attitude of the Negroes in the various places at which I had meetings.

Trotsky: I have not formed an opinion about the question because I do not have enough information. What Comrade James tells us now is very important. It shows that we can have some elements for cooperation in this field, but at the same time this information limits the immediate perspective of the organization. Who are those elements? The majority are Negro intellectuals, former Stalinist functionaries and sympathizers. We know that now large strata of the intellectuals are turning back to the Stalinists in every country. We have observed such people who were very sympathetic to us: Eastman, Solow, Hook,[25] and others. They were very sympathetic to us insofar as they considered us an object for their protection. They abandoned the Stalinists and looked for a new field of action, especially during the Moscow trials,[26] and so for the

---

25. Max Eastman (1883-1969) was a writer sympathetic to the Left Opposition in the 1920s and a translator of several Trotsky books. He broke with Marxism and later became an anticommunist and *Reader's Digest* editor. Herbert Solow (1903-1964) was a left-wing journalist who belonged briefly to the Workers Party, from 1934 to 1935, and helped defend Trotsky against Stalinist slander. He broke with Marxism and become a *Fortune* editor. Sidney Hook (1902-   ) was a professor who belonged to the American Workers Party before it merged with the CLA but dropped out soon after the Workers Party was started. During the cold war he became a supporter of the anticommunist witch-hunt and later a Nixonite.

26. Stalin's purges of his political opponents in the 1930s were highlighted by three Moscow trials—1936, 1937, and 1938—where the defend-

period they were our friends. Now since we have begun a vigorous campaign, they are hostile to us.

Many of them are returning to all sorts of vague things— humanism, etc. In France, Plisnier,[27] the famous author, went back to God as well as to democracy. But when the white intellectuals went back to Roosevelt and democracy, the disappointed Negro intellectuals looked for a new field on the basis of the Negro question. Of course we must utilize them, but they are not a basis for a large mass movement. They can be used only when there is a clear program and good slogans.

The real question is whether or not it is possible to organize a mass movement. You know for such disappointed elements we created FIARI.[28] It is not only for artists; anyone may enter. It is something of a moral or political "resort" for the disappointed intellectuals. Of course, it can also be used at times to protect us in certain ways, for money, to influence petty-bourgeois public opinion, and so on. That is one thing; but you consider these Negro intellectuals for the directing of a mass movement.

Your project would create something like a pre-political school. What determines the necessity? Two fundamental facts: that the large masses of the Negroes are backward and oppressed and this oppression is so strong that they must feel it every moment; that they feel it as Negroes. We must find the possibility of giving this feeling a political organizational expression. You may say that in Germany or in England we do not organize such semipolitical, semi-trade union, or semicultural organizations: we reply that we must adapt ourselves to the genuine Negro masses in the United States.

---

ants "confessed" participation in conspiracies with Nazi Germany and fascist Italy to restore capitalism in the USSR.

27. Charles Plisnier (1896-1952) was a Belgian writer who briefly belonged to the Left Opposition in the late 1920s.

28. FIARI was the International Federation of Revolutionary Writers and Artists, initiated in 1938. Its manifesto, "Towards a Free Revolutionary Art," signed by André Breton and Diego Rivera, was largely written by Trotsky and is reprinted in *Leon Trotsky on Literature and Art* (Pathfinder, 1970).

I will give you another example. We are terribly against the "French turn."[29] We abandoned our independence in order to penetrate into a centrist organization. You see that this Negro woman writes that they will not adhere to a Trotskyist organization. It is the result of the disappointments that they have had from the Stalinist organizations and also the propaganda of the Stalinists against us. They say, "We are already persecuted, just because we are Negroes. Now if we adhere to the Trotskyists, we will be even more oppressed."

Why did we penetrate into the Socialist Party and into the PSOP?[30] If we were not the left wing, subject to the most severe blows, our powers of attraction would be ten or a hundred times greater; the people would come to us. But now we must penetrate into other organizations, keeping our heads on our shoulders and telling them that we are not as bad as they say.

There is a certain analogy with the Negroes. They were enslaved by the whites. They were liberated by the whites (so-called liberation). They were led and misled by the whites, and they did not have their own political independence. They were in need of a pre-political activity as Negroes. Theoretically it seems to me absolutely clear that a special organization should be created for a special situation. The danger is only that it will become a game for the intellectuals. This organization can justify itself only by winning workers, sharecroppers, and so on. If it does not succeed, we will have to confess that it was a failure. If it does succeed we will be very happy, because we will have a mass organization of Negroes. In that case I fully agree with Comrade James, except of course with some reserva-

---

29. The "French turn" was a tactic, pursued by Fourth Internationalists in the mid-1930s, of joining the Socialist Party (in France and later the U.S.) in order to influence leftward-moving forces inside those parties and merge with them for the construction of a revolutionary party. Trotsky proposed this tactic. So when he said, "We are terribly against the 'French turn,'" he meant: It was not something we liked to do, even though we felt we had to do it.

30. The Workers and Peasants Socialist Party of France (PSOP) was a centrist group organized in 1938 after a left wing, led by Marceau Pivert, left the Socialist Party. It disintegrated when World War II began.

tions on the question of self-determination, as was stated in our other discussion.

The task is not one of simply passing through the organization for a few weeks. It is a question of awakening the Negro masses. It does not exclude recruitment. I believe that success is quite possible; I am not sure. But it is clear for us all that our comrades in such an organization should be organized into a group. We should take the initiative. I believe it is necessary. This supposes the adaptation of our transitional program[30] to the Negro problems in the States—a very carefully elaborated program with genuine civil rights, political rights, cultural interests, economic interests, and so on. It should be done.

I believe that there are two strata: the intellectuals and the masses. I believe that it is among the intellectuals that you find this opposition to self-determination. Why? Because they keep themselves separated from the masses, always with the desire to take on the Anglo-Saxon culture and of becoming an integral part of the Anglo-Saxon life. The majority are opportunists and reformists. Many of them continue to imagine that by the improvement of the mentality, and so on, the discrimination will disappear. That is why they are against any kind of sharp slogan.

James: They will maintain an intellectual interest because the Marxist analysis of Negro history and the problems of the day will give them an insight into the development of the Negroes which nothing else can. Also they are very much isolated from the white bourgeoisie, and the social discrimination makes them therefore less easily corrupted, as, for example, the Negro intellectuals in the West Indies. Furthermore, they are a very small section of the Negro population and on the whole are far less

31. The founding conference of the Fourth International in 1938 adopted a transitional program of demands and slogans designed to bridge the gap between the masses' level of consciousness and the needs of socialist revolution by drawing the masses into action around the demands and slogans. The 1938 program and Trotsky's thinking on transitional demands are included in *The Transitional Program for Socialist Revolution* (Pathfinder, 1977). The same book contains the SWP's 1969 resolution "A Transitional Program for Black Liberation."

dangerous than the corresponding section of the petty bourgeoisie in any other group or community. Also what has happened to the Jews in Germany has made the Negro intellectuals think twice. They will raise enough money to start the thing off. After that we do not have to bother in particular. Some, however, would maintain an intellectual interest and continue to give money.

Plans for the Negro Organization

Coyoacán, Mexico
April 11, 1939

James: The suggestions for the party work are in the documents and there is no need to go over them. I propose that they should be considered by the [SWP] Political Committee immediately, together with Comrade Trotsky's idea for a special number of the *New International*[32] on the Negro question. Urgently needed is a pamphlet written by someone familiar with the dealings of the CP on the Negro question and relating these to the Communist International and its degeneration. This would be an indispensable theoretical preliminary to the organization of the Negro movement and the party's own work among the Negroes. What is not needed is a general pamphlet dealing in a general way with the difficulties of the Negro and stating that in general black and white must unite. It would be another of a long list.

---

32. The SWP's theoretical magazine until 1940, when it was taken over by a group that split from the SWP. It was replaced in 1940 by *Fourth International,* which was renamed *International Socialist Review* in 1956. The *New International*'s "Special Negro Number" was dated December 1939.

The Negro Organization:
Theoretical:
1. The study of Negro history and historic propaganda should be:

(a) Emancipation of the Negroes in San Domingo linked with the French revolution.

(b) Emancipation of the slaves in the British Empire linked with the British Reform Bill of 1832.

(c) Emancipation of the Negroes in the United States linked with the Civil War in America.

This leads easily up to the conclusion that the emancipation of the Negro in the United States and abroad is linked with the emancipation of the white working class.

(d) The economic roots of racial discrimination.

(e) Fascism.

(f) The necessity for self-determination for Negro peoples in Africa and a similar policy in China, India, etc.

N.B.: The party should produce a theoretical study of the permanent revolution and the Negro peoples. This should be very different in style from the pamphlet previously suggested. It should not be a controversy with the CP, but a positive economic and political analysis showing that socialism is the only way out and definitely treating the theory on a high level. This however should come from the party.

2. A scrupulous analysis and exposure of the economic situation of the poorest Negroes and the way this retards not only the Negroes themselves, but the whole community. This, the bringing to the Negroes themselves of a formulated account of their own conditions by means of simple diagrams, illustrations, charts, etc., is of the utmost importance.

Theory—organizational means:
1. Weekly paper and pamphlets of the Negro organization.

2. To establish the *International African Opinion* as a monthly theoretical journal, financed to some degree from America, make it twice its present size and after a few months enter boldly upon a discussion of international socialism, emphasizing the right of self-determination,

taking care to show that socialism will be the decision of the Negro states themselves on the basis of their own experience. Invite an international participation of all organizations in the labor movement, Negro intellectuals, etc. It is to be hoped that Comrade Trotsky will be able to participate in this. This discussion on socialism should have no part in the weekly agitational paper.

Organizational:

1. Summon a small group of Negroes and whites if possible: Fourth Internationalists, Lovestoneites,[33] unattached revolutionaries—this group must be clear on (a) the war question and (b) socialism. We cannot begin by placing an abstract question like socialism before Negro workers. It seems to me that we cannot afford to have confusion on this question in the leaderhip; for it is on this question that hangs the whole direction of our day-to-day politics. Are we going to attempt to patch up capitalism or to break it? On the war question there can be no compromise. The Bureau has a position and that must be the basis of the new organization.

Program:

1. A careful adaptation of the program of the transitional demands with emphasis on the demands for equality. This is as much as can be said at present.

Practical steps:

1. Choose, after careful investigation, some trade union where there is discrimination affecting a large number of Negroes and where there is a possibility of success. Mobilize a national campaign with every conceivable means of united front: AFL, CIO, SP, SWP, Negro churches, bourgeois organizations and all, in an attempt to break down this discrimination. This should be the *first campaign,* to show clearly that the organization is fighting

---

33. A group headed by Jay Lovestone (1898-   ), which had been expelled from the American CP in 1929. It dissolved in 1940. Lovestone later became a rabid anticommunist and chief foreign policy adviser to the conservative AFL-CIO bureaucracy.

as a Negro organization, but has nothing to do with Garveyism.

2. To seek to build a nationwide organization on Negro housing and high rents, attempting to draw the women in for militant action.

3. Discrimination in restaurants should be fought by a campaign. A number of Negroes in any area go into a restaurant all together, ordering for instance some coffee, and refuse to come out until they are served. It would be possible to sit there for a whole day in a very orderly manner and throw upon the police the necessity of removing these Negroes. A campaign to be built around such action.

4. The question of the organization of domestic servants is very important and though very difficult a thorough investigation should be made.

5. Negro unemployment—though here great care will have to be taken to avoid duplicating organizations; and this is probably the role of the party.

6. The Negro organization must take the sharecroppers' organization in the South as its own. It must make it one of the bases of the solution of the Negro question in the South; popularize its work, its aims, its possibilities in the East and West; try to influence it in a more militant direction; invite speakers from it; urge it to take action against lynching; and make the whole Negro community and the whites aware of its importance in the regional and national struggle.

Political orientation:

1. To initiate a militant struggle against fascism and to see to it that Negroes are always in the forefront of any demonstration or activity against fascism.

2. To inculcate the impossibility of any assistance being gained from the Republican and Democratic parties. Negroes must put up their own candidates on a working class program and form a united front only with those candidates whose program approximates theirs.

Internal organization:
The local units will devote themselves to these questions

in accordance with the urgency of the local situation and the national campaigns planned by the center. These can only be decided upon by investigation.

(a) Begin with a large-scale campaign for funds to establish a paper and at least two headquarters—one in New York and one in a town like St. Louis, within striking distance of the South.

(b) A weekly agitational paper costing two cents.

(c) The aim should be to have as soon as possible at least five professional revolutionists—two in New York, two in St. Louis (?), and one constantly traveling from the center. A national tour in the fall after the paper has been established and a draft program and aims established. A national conference in the early summer.

(d) Seek to get a Negro militant from South Africa to make a tour here as soon as possible. There is little doubt that this can easily be arranged.

The party members in the organization will form a fraction, and all important documents submitted by the fraction to the Negro organization must be ratified either by the Political Committee or its appointed representatives.

Curtiss: About opening the discussion of socialism in the bulletin [the proposed theoretical journal], but excluding it, at least for a time, from the weekly paper: it seems to me that this is dangerous. This is falling into the idea that socialism is for intellectuals and the elite, but that the people on the bottom should be interested only in the common, day-to-day things. The method should be different in both places, but I think that there should at least be a drive in the direction of socialism in the weekly paper not only from the point of view of daily matters but also in what we call abstract discussion. It is a contradiction—the mass paper would have to take a clear position on the war question, but not on socialism. It is impossible to do the first without the second. It is a form of economism [that] the workers should interest themselves in the everyday affairs, but not in the theories of socialism.

James: I see the difficulties and the contradiction, but there is something else that I cannot quite see—if we want to build a mass movement we cannot plunge into a discussion of socialism, because I think that it would cause more confusion than it would gain support. The Negro is not interested in socialism. He can be brought to socialism on the basis of his concrete experiences. Otherwise we would have to form a Negro socialist organization. I think we must put forth a minimal, concrete program. I agree that we should not put socialism too far in the future, but I am trying to avoid lengthy discussions on Marxism, the Second International, the Third International, etc.

Lankin:[34] Would this organization throw its doors open to all classes of Negroes?

James: Yes, on the basis of its program. The bourgeois Negro can come in to help, but only on the basis of the organization's program.

Lankin: I cannot see how the Negro bourgeoisie can help the Negro proletariat fight for its economic advancement.

James: In our own movement some of us are petty bourgeois. If a bourgeois Negro is excluded from a university because of his color, this organization will probably mobilize the masses to fight for the rights of the bourgeois Negro student. Help for the organization will be mobilized on the basis of its program, and we will not be able to exclude any Negro from it if he is willing to fight for that program.

Trotsky: I believe that the first question is the attitude of the Socialist Workers Party toward the Negroes. It is very disquieting to find that until now the party has done almost nothing in this field. It has not published a book, a pamphlet, leaflets, nor even any articles in the *New International.* Two comrades who compiled a book on the question, a serious work, remained isolated.[35] That book is not published, nor are even quotations from it published. It is not a good sign. It is a bad sign. The characteristic thing

---

34. Sol Lankin was one of the founders of the American Left Opposition, serving as a guard in Trotsky's home in 1939.

35. The two authors were Barney Mayes and William Bennett, and their 250-page study was entitled "The Negro in the U.S." It was never published anywhere.

about the American workers' parties, trade union organizations, and so on, was their aristocratic character. It is the basis of opportunism. The skilled workers who feel set in the capitalist society help the bourgeois class to hold the Negroes and the unskilled workers down to a very low scale. Our party is not safe from degeneration if it remains a place for intellectuals, semi-intellectuals, skilled workers, and Jewish workers who build a very close milieu which is almost isolated from the genuine masses. Under these conditions our party cannot develop—it will degenerate.

We must have this great danger before our eyes. Many times I have proposed that every member of the party, especially the intellectuals and semi-intellectuals, who, during a period of say six months, cannot each win a worker-member for the party should be demoted to the position of sympathizer. We can say the same in the Negro question. The old organizations, beginning with the AFL, are the organizations of the workers' aristocracy. Our party is a part of the same milieu, not of the basic exploited masses of whom the Negroes are the most exploited. The fact that our party until now has not turned to the Negro question is a very disquieting symptom. If the workers' aristocracy is the basis of opportunism, one of the sources of adaptation to capitalist society, then the most oppressed and discriminated are the most dynamic milieu of the working class.

We must say to the conscious elements of the Negroes that they are convoked by the historic development to become a vanguard of the working class. What serves as the brake on the higher strata? It is the privileges, the comforts that hinder them from becoming revolutionists. It does not exist for the Negroes. What can transform a certain stratum, make it more capable of courage and sacrifice? It is concentrated in the Negroes. If it happens that we in the SWP are not able to find the road to this stratum, then we are not worthy at all. The permanent revolution and all the rest would be only a lie.

In the States we now have various contests. Competition to see who will sell the most papers, and so on. That is very good. But we must also establish a more serious competition—the recruiting of workers and especially of Negro workers. To a certain degree that is independent of the creation of the special Negro organization.

I believe the party should utilize the sojourn of Comrade James in the States (the tour was necessary to acquaint him with conditions) but now for the next six months, for a behind-the-scenes organizational and political work in order to avoid attracting too much attention from the authorities. A six months' program can be elaborated for the Negro question, so that if James should be obliged to return to Great Britain, for personal reasons or through the pressure of the police, after a half year's work we have a base for the Negro movement and we have a serious nucleus of Negroes and whites working together on this plan. It is a question of the vitality of the party. It is an important question. It is a question of whether the party is to be transformed into a sect or if it is capable of finding its way to the most oppressed part of the working class.

*   *   *

Proposals taken up point by point:

1. Pamphlet on the Negro question and the Negroes in the CP, relating it to the degeneration of the Kremlin.

Trotsky: Good. And also would it not be well perhaps to mimeograph this book, or parts of it, and send it together with other material on the question to the various sections of the party for discussion?

2. A Negro number of the *New International*.

Trotsky: I believe that it is absolutely necessary.

Owen: It seems to me that there is a danger of getting out the Negro number before we have a sufficient Negro organization to assure its distribution.

James: It is not intended primarily for the Negroes. It is intended for the party itself and for the other readers of the theoretical magazine.

3. The use of the history of the Negroes themselves in educating them.

General agreement.

4. A study of the permanent revolution and the Negro question.

General agreement.

5. The question of socialism—whether to bring it in through the paper or through the bulletin [the proposed theoretical journal].

Trotsky: I do not believe that we can begin with the exclusion of socialism from the organization. You propose a very large, somewhat heterogeneous organization, which will also accept religious people. That would signify that if a Negro worker, or farmer, or merchant, makes a speech in the organization to the effect that the only salvation for the Negroes is in the church, we will be too tolerant to expel him and at the same time so wise that we will not let him speak in favor of religion, but we will not speak in favor of socialism.[36] If we understand the character of this milieu, we will adapt the presentation of our ideas to it. We will be cautious; but to tie our hands in advance—to say that we will not introduce the question of socialism because it is an abstract matter—that is not possible. It is one thing to present a general socialist program; and another thing to be very attentive to the concrete questions of Negro life and to oppose socialism to capitalism in these questions. It is one thing to accept a heterogeneous group and to work in it, and another to be absorbed by it.

James: I quite agree with what you say. What I am afraid of is the putting forth of an abstract socialism. You will recall that I said that the leading group must clearly understand what it is doing and where it is going. But the socialist education of the masses should arise from the day-to-day questions. I am only anxious to prevent the thing's developing into an endless discussion. The discussion should be free and thorough in the theoretical organ.

In regard to the question of socialism in the agitational organ, it is my view that the organization should definitely establish itself as doing the day-to-day work of the Negroes in such a way that the masses of Negroes can take part in

---

36. The meaning of this sentence is clearer if it is understood that Trotsky was in part speaking sarcastically.

it before involving itself in discussions about socialism. While it is clear that an individual can raise whatever points he wishes and point out his solution of the Negro problems, yet the question is whether those who are guiding the organization as a whole should begin by speaking in the name of socialism. I think not. It is important to remember that those who take the initiative should have some common agreement as to the fundamentals of politics today, otherwise there will be great trouble as the organization develops. But although these, as individuals, are entitled to put forward their particular point of view in the general discussion, yet the issue is whether they should speak as a body as socialists from the very beginning, and my personal view is no.

Trotsky: In the theoretical organ you can have theoretical discussion, and in the mass organ you can have a mass political discussion. You say that they are contaminated by the capitalist propaganda. Say to them, "You don't believe in socialism. But you will see that in the fighting, the members of the Fourth International will not only be with you, but possibly the most militant." I would even go so far as to have every one of our speakers end his speech by saying, "My name is the Fourth International!" They will come to see that we are the fighters, while the person who preaches religion in the hall, in the critical moment, will go to the church instead of to the battlefield.

6. The organizing groups and individuals of the new organization must be in complete agreement on the war question.

Trotsky: Yes, it is the most important and the most difficult question. The program may be very modest, but at the same time it must leave to everyone his freedom of expression in his speeches, and so on; the program must not be the limitation of our activity, but only our common obligation. Everyone must have the right to go further, but everyone is obliged to defend the minimum. We will see how this minimum will be crystallized as we go along in the opening steps.

7. A campaign in some industry in behalf of the Negroes.

Trotsky: That is important. It will bring a conflict with some white workers who will not want it. It is a shift from the most aristocratic workers' elements to the lowest elements. We attracted to ourselves some of the higher strata of the intellectuals when they felt that we needed protection: Dewey, La Follette,[37] etc. Now that we are undertaking serious work, they are leaving us. I believe that we will lose two or three more strata and go more deeply into the masses. This will be the touchstone.

8. Housing and rent campaign.

Trotsky: It is absolutely necessary.

Curtiss: It also works in very well with our transitional demands.

9. The demonstration in the restaurant.

Trotsky: Yes, and give it an even more militant character. There could be a picket line outside to attract attention and explain something of what is going on.

10. Domestic servants.

Trotsky: Yes, I believe it is very important; but I believe that there is the *a priori* consideration that many of these Negroes are servants for rich people and are demoralized and have been transformed into moral lackeys. But there are others, a larger stratum, and the question is to win those who are not so privileged.

Owen: That is a point that I wished to present. Some years ago I was living in Los Angeles near a Negro section—one set aside from the others. The Negroes there were more prosperous. I inquired as to their work and was told by the Negroes themselves that they were better off because they were servants—many of them in the houses of the movie colony. I was surprised to find the servants in the higher strata. This colony of Negroes was not small—it consisted of several thousand people.

---

37. John Dewey (1859-1952), the American educator and philosopher, and Suzanne La Follette (1893-   ), former editor of the *New Freeman,* were chairman and secretary, respectively, of the Commission of Inquiry into the Charges Made Against Leon Trotsky in the Moscow Trials, also called the Dewey Commission. The summary of the commission's findings was published in *Not Guilty* (reprinted by Monad Press, 1972). A controversy between Dewey and Trotsky about morality is presented in *Their Morals and Ours* (Pathfinder, 1973).

James: That is true. But if you are serious, it is not difficult to get to the Negro masses. They live together and they feel together. This stratum of privileged Negroes is smaller than any other privileged stratum. The whites treat them with such contempt that in spite of themselves they are closer to the other Negroes than you would think. In the West Indies, for example, there are great divisions among the Negroes—certain classes of Negroes do not fraternize with other classes. But that is not true here. Here they are kept in the ghetto.

11. Mobilize the Negroes against fascism.
General agreement.

12. The relationship of the Negroes to the Republican and Democratic parties.

Trotsky: How many Negroes are there in Congress? One. There are 440 members in the House of Representatives and 96 in the Senate. Then if the Negroes have almost 10 percent of the population, they are entitled to 50 members, but they have only one. It is a clear picture of political inequality. We can often oppose a Negro candidate to a white candidate. This Negro organization can always say, "We want a Negro who knows our problems." It can have important consequences.

Owen: It seems to me that Comrade James has ignored a very important part of our program—the labor party.

James: The Negro section wants to put up a Negro candidate. We tell them they must not stand just as Negroes, but they must have a program suitable to the masses of poor Negroes. They are not stupid and they can understand that and it is to be encouraged. The white workers put up a labor candidate in another section. Then we say to the Negroes in the white section, "Support that candidate, because his demands are good workers' demands." And we say to the white workers in the Negro area, "You should support the Negro candidate, because although he is a Negro you will notice that his demands are good for the whole working class." This means that the Negroes have the satisfaction of having their own candidates in areas where they predominate and at the same time we build labor solidarity. It fits into the labor party program.

Curtiss: Isn't that coming close to the People's Front, to vote for a Negro just because he is a Negro?

James: This organization has a program. When the Democrats put up a Negro candidate, we say, "Not at all. It must be a candidate with a program we can support."

Trotsky: It is a question of another organization for which we are not responsible, just as they are not responsible for us. If this organization puts up a certain candidate, and we find as a party that we must put up our own candidate in opposition, we have the full right to do so. If we are weak and cannot get the organization to choose a revolutionist, and they choose a Negro Democrat, we might even withdraw our candidate with a concrete declaration that we abstain from fighting, not the Democrat, but the Negro. We consider that the Negro's candidacy as opposed to the white's candidacy, even if both are of the same party, is an important factor in the struggle of the Negroes for their equality; and in this case we can critically support them. I believe that it can be done in certain instances.[38]

13. A Negro from South or West Africa to tour the States.

Trotsky: What will he teach?

James: I have in mind several young Negroes, any one of whom can give a clear anti-imperialist, antiwar picture. I think it would be very important in building up an understanding of internationalism.

14. Submit documents and plans to the Political Committee.

General agreement.

---

38. What Trotsky was proposing here was that the SWP give critical support to the candidate of an independent Negro organization running against the Democratic and Republican party candidates, even though the candidate might be a Democrat instead of a revolutionist. The crucial point would be that such a candidate of an independent Negro organization would be opposing the candidates of the capitalist parties. Trotsky never advocated support of candidates of the Democratic or Republican parties.

James: I agree with your attitude on the party work in connection with the Negroes. They are a tremendous force and they will dominate the whole of the Southern states. If the party gets a hold here, the revolution is won in America. Nothing can stop it.

APPENDIX A

Results of the Discussions

The transcripts of the three discussions in Mexico were submitted in an internal bulletin to the membership of the SWP for discussion prior to their approaching national convention, held in New York City, July 1-4, 1939. On July 3, a convention Committee on Negro Work presented to the delegates a program of action which the convention referred to the incoming National Committee for implementation. It also presented two resolutions. The first, entitled "The SWP and Negro Work," was adopted without opposition. Its text follows:

The SWP and Negro Work

The American Negroes, for centuries the most oppressed section of American society and the most discriminated against, are potentially the most revolutionary element of the population. They are designated by their whole historical past to be, under adequate leadership, the very vanguard of the proletarian revolution.[*] The neglect of Negro work and of the Negro question by the party is therefore a very disquieting sign. The SWP must recognize that its attitude to the Negro question is crucial for its future development. Hitherto the party has been based mainly on privileged workers and groups of isolated intellectuals. Unless it

---

[*]C. L. R. James, the principal author of this resolution, wrote a column about this sentence in the SWP paper, *Socialist Appeal,* August 22, 1939. Under the pen name of "J. R. Johnson," he said at one point, "There is, in the sentence quoted, an overstatement, in my opinion. It would be more correct to say, 'in the very vanguard.'" No one else on the Committee on Negro Work or in the SWP leadership expressed any differences with James's opinion. For a comment in 1964, see *How a Minority Can Change Society,* by George Breitman (Pathfinder, 1975).

can find its way to the great masses of the underprivileged, of whom the Negroes constitute so important a section, the broad perspectives of the permanent revolution will remain only a fiction and the party is bound to degenerate.

The SWP proposes therefore to constitute a National Negro Department which will initiate and coordinate a plan of work among the Negroes and calls upon its members to cooperate strenuously in the difficult task of approaching this work in the most suitable manner. Our obvious tasks for the coming period are (a) the education of the party, (b) winning the politically more advanced Negroes for the Fourth International, and (c) through the work of the party among the Negroes and in wider fields influencing the Negro masses to recognize in the SWP the only party which is genuinely working for their complete emancipation from the heavy burdens they have borne so long. The winning of masses of Negroes to our movement on a revolutionary basis is, however, no easy task. The Negroes, suffering acutely from the general difficulties of all workers under capitalism, and in addition, from special problems of their own, are naturally hesitant to take the step of allying themselves with a small and heavily persecuted party. But Negro work is complicated by other, more profound, causes. For reasons which can be easily understood, the American Negro is profoundly suspicious of all whites, and recent events have deepened that suspicion.

In the past, the Negro masses have had disastrous experiences with the Republican and Democratic parties. The benefits that the Negroes as a whole are supposed to have received from the New Deal and the Democratic Party can easily be seen for the fraud that they are when it is recognized that it is the Democratic Party of Franklin Roosevelt which by force and trickery prevents the Negroes from exercising their votes over large areas in the South.

The CP of the USA from 1928 to 1935 did win a number of Negroes to membership and awakened a sympathetic interest among the politically more advanced Negro workers and intellectuals. But the bureaucratic creation of Negro "leaders," their subservience to the twists and turns of the party line, their slavish dependence on the manipulations and combinations of the CP leadership, were seen by interested Negroes not as a transference of the methods and practices of the Kremlin bureaucracy to America, but merely as another example of the use of Negroes by whites for political purposes unconnected with Negro struggles. With its latest turn beginning in 1935, the CP has become openly a party of American bourgeois democracy. Not only to expand, but merely to exist in this milieu demanded that it imbibe and practice the racial discriminations inherent in that society. The Negroes, very sensitive to all such practices, have quickly recognized the new face of the CP beneath the mask of demagogy with which it seeks to disguise the predicament in which it finds itself, and the result has been a mass departure from the party (80 percent of the New York State Negro membership) and a bitter hostility to the CP, which reached a climax when well-known former Negro members of the CP testified against it before the Dies [House Un-American Activities] Committee. Once more the Third International has struck a deadly blow at the American working class, this time by undermining the confidence that was being slowly forged between the politically advanced sections of the black and white workers.

Furthermore, the awakening political consciousness of the Negro not unnaturally takes the form of a desire for independent action uncontrolled by whites. The Negroes have long felt and more than ever feel today the urge to create their own organizations under their own leaders and thus assert, not only in theory but in action, their claim to complete equality with other American citizens. Such a desire is legitimate and must be vigorously supported even when it takes the form of a rather aggressive chauvinism. Black chauvinism in America today is merely the natural excess of the desire for equality and is essentially progressive while white American chauvinism, the expression of racial domination, is essentially reactionary. Under any circumstances, it would have been a task of profound difficulty, perhaps impossible, for a revolutionary party composed mainly of whites to win the confidence of the American Negro masses, except in the actual crises of revolutionary struggles. Such possibilities as existed, however, have been gravely undermined by the CP. Today the politically minded Negroes are turning away from the CP, and Negro organizations devoted to struggle for Negro rights are springing up all over the North and East, particularly in Harlem. The nationalist tendencies of the Negroes have been fortified, and in addition to the poisoning of racial relations by capitalism, the SWP has now to contend with the heritage left by the CP and the pernicious course it is still actively pursuing.

The SWP therefore proposes that its Negro members, aided and supported by the party, take the initiative and collaborate with other militant Negroes in the formation of a Negro mass organization devoted to the struggle for Negro rights. *This organization will NOT be either openly or secretly a periphery organization of the Fourth International.* It will be an organization in which the masses of Negroes will be invited to participate on a working class program corresponding to the day-to-day struggles of the masses of Negro workers and farmers. Its program will be elaborated by the Negro organization, in which Negro members of the Fourth International will participate with neither greater nor lesser rights than other members. But the SWP is confident that the position of the Negroes in American society, the logic of the class struggle in the present period, the superior grasp of politics and the morale of members of the Fourth International, must inevitably result in its members exercising a powerful influence in such an organization. The support of such an organization by the SWP does not in any way limit the party's drive among Negroes for membership, neither does it invalidate the necessary struggle for the unity of both black and white workers. But that road is not likely to be a broad highway. Such an organization as is proposed is the most likely means of bringing the masses of Negroes into political action, which, though programmatically devoted to their own interests, must inevitably merge with the broader struggles of the American working class movement taken as a whole. The SWP, therefore, while recognizing the limitations and pitfalls of a mass organization without clearly defined political program, and while retaining its full liberty of action and criticism, welcomes and supports any attempt by Negroes themselves to organize for militant action against our common oppressors, instructs its Negro members to work actively toward the formation of such an organization, and recommends to the party members to follow closely all such manifestations of Negro militancy.

> Adopted by the Socialist
> Workers Party convention,
> July 3, 1939

The second resolution was entitled "The Right of Self-Determination and the Negro in the United States of North America." The overwhelming majority of the Committee on Negro Work recommended its adoption, but two members had differences with it, and they were permitted to present their minority reports to the convention. The minority reports received little support from the delegates, who voted to adopt the resolution "as a basis for a final draft," to constitute one part of a broader, more general resolution dealing with all aspects of the Negro struggle. Its text follows:

The Right of Self-Determination and the Negro in the United States of North America

In 1930 Negroes in America constituted nearly twelve million, or 10 percent, of the American population. Of these, two-thirds were still in the South, despite the war and postwar emigration to the North. In the cities of the North and East, the Negroes form only a small minority of the population, generally less than 10 percent. In the cities of the South the proportion is much higher, but in only one large city, Birmingham, Alabama, do the Negroes constitute as much as one half of the white population. Similarly in the state areas of the South, they are outnumbered by the whites. In only one state of America, Mississippi, are the Negroes in a majority, and that of only 2 percent, though there are large county areas inhabited by a majority of Negroes.

Cut off for centuries from all contact with the continent and customs of his origin, the Negro is today an American citizen. In his daily work, language, religion, and general culture he differs not at all from his fellow workers in factory and field, except in the intensity of his exploitation and the attendant brutal discrimination. These discriminations are imposed by capitalism in the pretended name of the Negro's racial characteristics, but in reality to increase profit by cheapening labor and to weaken the workers and farmers by fostering racial rivalries.

The minority status of the Negro in the political divisions of capitalist America, even in the South, and the absence of a national Negro language and literature and of a differentiated political history, as in prewar Poland or Catalonia and the Ukraine of today, have caused in the past a too facile acceptance of the Negroes as merely a more than usually oppressed section of the American workers and farmers. This in turn has led to a neglect of the Negro's political past and a lack of historical imagination in envisaging his future political development.

The American Negroes were among the earliest colonists of America, and for three centuries their history has been one of continual economic exploitation, social discrimination, and political expropriation by all classes of whites. Up to 1935, organized labor as represented by the AFL discriminated against the Negro as sharply as the capitalist class; today the poor whites of the South are the most savage of lynchers and the most rabid upholders of the theory of white superiority. The world economic crisis and consequent organization of the CIO including hundreds of thousands of Negroes, the organization of the Southern Tenant Farmers Union comprising both white and black, have shown that this division between the black and white workers is beginning to close under economic pressure. But not even a socialist revolution can immediately destroy the accumulated memories, mistrust, and suspicions of centuries; and today, in this period of capitalistic decline in America, the racial prejudices are more than ever based on economic privileges, possessed by one group of workers at the obvious and immediate expense of the other. Negroes today are being pushed out of jobs which, before the depression, whites disdained. Three centuries of property and privilege have used their wealth and power to make the Negroes feel they are and must continue to be outcasts from all sections of American society, rich and poor; and the political backwardness of the American working class movement has made it an easy victim to this propaganda, fortified by tangible if slight economic advantages. It is not improbable, therefore, that the bulk of the Negroes have absorbed their lesson far more profoundly than is superficially apparent and that on their first political awakening to the necessity of revolutionary activity they may demand the right of self-determination, i.e., the formation of a Negro state in the South. Thus, in their view, they would be free from that exploitation, discrimination and arrogance, inseparable in their experience from any association with numerically superior whites. The desire to wipe out the humiliating political subservience and social degradation of centuries might find expression in an overpowering demand for the establishment and administration of a Negro state.

The past political history of the Negroes gives not insignificant indications that their political development may very well follow this course. The Garvey movement, one of the most powerful political mass movements ever seen in the USA, concealed behind its fantastic and reactionary slogan of "Back to Africa" the desire (revolutionary in its essence) for a Negro state. The Negroes no more desired to go to Africa of their own free will than German Jews before Hitler wanted to go to Palestine. The masses of Negroes, particularly in the South, dominated by the heritage of slavery and the apparently irresistible numbers and state power of the whites, did not dare to raise the slogan of a black state in America. But in a revolutionary crisis, as they begin to shake off the state coercion and ideological domination of American bourgeois society, their first step may well be to demand the control, both actual and symbolical, of their own future destiny. The question of whether the Negroes in America are a national minority to which the slogan of self-determination applies will be solved in practice. The raising or support of the slogan by the masses of Negroes will be the best and only proof required. It is inconceivable that propaganda by any American revolutionary party can instill this idea into their minds if they did not themselves consciously or unconsciously desire it. This desire may very well fall into the hands of reactionary leaders. But only the most energetic defense of the right of self-determination of the Negro masses can lead their movement into revolutionary channels.

Should the masses of Negroes raise this slogan, the SWP, in accordance with the Leninist doctrine on the question of self-determination and the imperative circumstances of the particular situation, will welcome this awakening and pledge itself to support the demand to the fullest extent of its power. The boundaries of such a state will be a matter of comradely arrangement between different sections of a revolution victorious over American capitalism and intent only on creating the best possible milieu for the building of the socialist commonwealth. The Fourth International aims at the abolition of the old and not at the creation of new national boundaries, but the historical circumstances and the stages of development of different sections of society will at given moments be decisive in the road to be followed at a particular historic moment. The demand for a Negro state in America, its revolutionary achievement with the enthusiastic encouragement and assistance of the whites, will generate such creative energy in every section of the Negro workers and farmers in America as to constitute a great step forward to the ultimate integration of the American Negroes into the United Socialist States of North America. The SWP is also confident that after a few years of independent existence the victories of the new regime in both states will lead inevitably to a unity, with the Negroes as anxious and willing partners, their justifiable suspicions and doubts weakened by the concrete manifestation of the desire for collaboration by the whites and the contrast between the capitalist and the socialist state. Such a development in America will have immediate and powerful repercussions not only among the millions of African Negroes but also among oppressed nationalities, particularly of color, everywhere, and will be a powerful step toward the dissolution of those national and racial antagonisms with which capitalism, particularly in this period of its desperate crisis, is poisoning and corrupting human society.

The SWP, while proclaiming its willingness to support the right of self-determination to the fullest degree, will not in itself, in the present stage, advocate the slogan of a Negro state in the manner of the Communist Party of the USA. The advocacy of the *right* of self-determination does not mean advancing the *slogan* of self-determination. Self-determination for Negroes means that the Negroes themselves must determine their own future. Furthermore, a party predominantly white in membership which, in present-day America, vigorously advocates such a slogan, prejudices it in the minds of Negroes, who see it as a form of segregation. But the SWP will watch carefully the political development of the masses of the Negroes, will emphasize their right to make this important decision themselves and the obligation of all revolutionaries to support whatever decision the Negroes may finally come to as to the necessity of a Negro state. The SWP recognizes that the Negroes have not yet expressed themselves on this important question. The opposition to a Negro state comes mainly from the articulate and vocal but small and weak class of Negro intellectuals, concerned with little else besides gaining a place for themselves in American capitalist society, and fanatically blind to its rapid decline. Negro members of the Fourth International, however, have every right to participate in the formation of the ideology of their own race, with such slogans and propaganda as correspond to the political development and revolutionary awakening of the great masses of the Negro people; and, while conscious of the ultimate aims of socialism, must recognize the progressive and revolutionary character of any demand unfolding among great masses of

Negroes for a Negro state, and if necessary vigorously advocate it.

> Adopted by the Socialist
> Workers Party convention,
> July 3, 1939, as the basis for
> a final draft to be prepared by
> the SWP National Committee

If not completely identical, the views of Trotsky and the Socialist Workers Party were now similar. The resolutions adopted at the SWP's 1939 convention, the most advanced application of Marxism to race relations that any American party had made, stimulated and prepared the SWP to play a leading role in the struggles against racism during and after World War II. They also laid the groundwork for the SWP to present the only consistently revolutionary attitude to black nationalism when that tendency began to assume mass proportions in the 1960s. (See the SWP's 1963 convention resolution, Freedom Now: The New Stage in the Struggle for Negro Emancipation, *Pioneer Publishers, 1963.)*

APPENDIX B

Trotsky on National
and Racial Oppression
(Excerpts)

The Feeling of Human Dignity

In 1923, before he recognized the national aspects of the American Negro struggle, Trotsky was asked some questions by the then revolutionary black poet, Claude McKay (1889-1948). The final part of his reply, written in Moscow, said:

The education of Negro propagandists is an exceedingly urgent and important revolutionary task at the present juncture.

In North America the matter is further complicated by the abominable obtuseness and caste presumptions of the privileged upper strata of the working class itself, who refuse to recognize fellow workers and fighting comrades in the Negroes. [AFL President Samuel] Gompers's policy is founded on the exploitation of such despicable prejudices, and is at the present time the most effective guarantee for the successful subjugation of white and colored workers alike. The fight against this policy must be taken up from different sides, and conducted on various lines. One of the most important branches of this conflict consists in enlightening the proletarian consciousness by awakening the feeling of human dignity, and of revolutionary protest, among the Negro slaves of American capitalism. As stated above, this work can only be carried out by self-sacrificing and politically educated revolutionary Negroes.

Needless to say, the work is not to be carried out in a spirit of Negro chauvinism, which would then merely form a counterpart of white chauvinism—but in a spirit of solidarity of all exploited without consideration of color.

What forms of organization are most suitable for the movement among American Negroes, it is difficult for me to say. as I am

81

insufficiently informed regarding the concrete conditions and possibilities. But the forms of organization will be found, as soon as there is sufficient will to action.

"A Letter to Comrade McKay," reprinted in
The First Five Years of American Communism, vol. 2, 1945

The Level Where National Aspirations Begin

One reason why Trotsky believed that American Negroes might develop nationalist and separatist aspirations in a revolutionary situation, when they would "feel that the domination by the whites is terminated," was that he had witnessed a similar development in the Russian empire in the revolutionary year of 1917. Among the oppressed nationalities in that empire there were several that did not raise nationalist demands until the czarist regime was overthrown in the February revolution, and others that did not raise them until the October (Bolshevik) revolution, or after:

When Rosa Luxemburg, in her posthumous polemic against the program of the October revolution, asserted that Ukrainian nationalism, having been formerly a mere "amusement" of the commonplace petty-bourgeois intelligentsia, had been artificially raised up by the yeast of the Bolshevik formula of self-determination, she fell, notwithstanding her luminous mind, into a very serious historic error. The Ukrainian peasantry had not made national demands in the past for the reason that the Ukrainian peasantry had not in general risen to the height of political being. The chief service of the February revolution—perhaps its only service, but one amply sufficient—lay exactly in this, that it gave the oppressed classes and nations of Russia at last an opportunity to speak out. . . .

Their general economic and cultural primitiveness did not permit the Siberian outlanders—kept down as they were both by nature and exploitation—to rise even to that level where national aspirations begin. . . .

The peoples and tribes along the Volga, in the northern Caucasus, in central Asia—awakened for the first time out of their prehistoric existence by the February revolution—had as yet neither national bourgeoisie nor national proletariat.

The History of the Russian Revolution, vol. 3, 1932

Stalin Completely Forgets

Prior to Lenin's contention that American Negroes were an oppressed minority, Stalin did not display much understanding of the degree of national oppression in the United States. This was Trotsky's comment on an article written by Stalin in 1917:

On March 25, in an article dealing with a government decree on the abolition of national limitations, Stalin tried to formulate the national question on a historic scale. "The social basis of national oppression," he writes, "the power inspiring it, is a decaying landed aristocracy." The fact that national oppression developed unprecedentedly during the epoch of capitalism, and found its most barbaric expression in colonial policies, seems to be beyond the ken of the democratic author. "In England," he continues, "where the landed aristocracy shares the power with the bourgeoisie, where the unlimited power of this aristocracy long ago ceased to exist, national oppression is milder, less inhumane—leaving out of account, of course, the circumstance that during the war, when the power has gone over into the hands of the landlords [!], national oppression was considerably strengthened (persecution of Ireland and India)." Those guilty of oppressing Ireland and India are the landlords, who—evidently in the person of Lloyd George—have seized the power thanks to the war. ". . . In Switzerland and North America," continues Stalin, "where there is no landlordism and never has been [!], where the power is undivided in the hands of the bourgeoisie, nationalities have developed freely. National oppression, generally speaking, finds no place. . . ." The author completely forgets the Negro, Indian, immigrant and colonial problems in the United States.

The History of the Russian Revolution, vol. 3, 1932

To Whom Belongs the Decisive Word

In 1932, twenty-four black South Africans ("and others") in Johannesburg, South Africa, sent a letter to the Left Opposition, asking questions about its program and applying for membership. From Prinkipo, Trotsky wrote a letter, which said in part:

The Johannesburg comrades may not as yet have had the opportunity to acquaint themselves more closely with the views of the Left Opposition on all the most important questions. But this cannot be an obstacle to our getting together with them as closely as possible at this very moment, and helping them in a comradely way to come into the orbit of our program and our tactics.

When ten intellectuals, whether in Paris, Berlin, or New York, who have already been members of various organizations, address themselves to us with a request to be taken into our midst, I would offer the following advice: put them through a series of tests on all the programmatic questions; wet them in the rain, dry them in the sun, and then after a new and careful examination accept maybe one or two.

The case is radically altered when ten workers connected with the masses turn to us. The difference in our attitude to a petty-bourgeois group and to the proletarian group does not require any explanation. But if a proletarian group functions in an area where there are workers of different races and, in spite of this, remains composed solely of workers of a privileged nationality, then I am inclined to view them with suspicion. Are we not dealing perhaps with the labor aristocracy? Isn't the group infected with slaveholding prejudices, active or passive?

It is an entirely different matter when we are approached by a group of Negro workers. Here I am prepared to take it for granted in advance that we shall achieve agreement with them, even if such an agreement is not yet evident, because the Negro workers, by virtue of their whole position, do not and cannot strive to degrade anybody, oppress anybody, or deprive anybody of his rights. They do not seek privileges and cannot rise to the top except on the road of the international revolution.

We can and we must find a way to the consciousness of the Negro workers, the Chinese workers, the Indian workers, and all the oppressed in the human ocean of the colored races to whom belongs the decisive word in the development of mankind.

"Closer to the Proletarians of the 'Colored' Races,"
June 13, 1932, reprinted in *Writings of Leon Trotsky (1932)*

The National Character of a Social Revolution

In 1935, Trotsky wrote a letter about a programmatic document ("theses") that had been prepared and was being discussed by a group of Left Oppositionists in South Africa. Trotsky said he had no differences in principle with the document, but felt it contained certain exaggerations and inaccuracies that should be corrected in the final draft of the document:

The South African possessions of Great Britain form a dominion only from the point of view of the white minority. From the point of the black majority, South Africa is a slave colony. . . . Three-quarters of the population of South Africa (almost six million of the almost eight million total) is composed of non-Europeans. . . .

Under these conditions the South African Republic will emerge first of all as a "black" republic; this does not exclude, of course, either full equality for the whites, or brotherly relations between the two races—depending mainly on the conduct of the whites. But it is entirely obvious that the predominant majority of the population, liberated from slavish dependence, will put a certain imprint on the state.

Insofar as a victorious revolution will radically change not only the relations between the classes but also between the races, and will assure to the blacks that place in the state which corresponds to their numbers, insofar will the *social* revolution in South Africa also have a *national* character.

We have not the slightest reason to close our eyes to this side of the question or to diminish its significance. On the contrary, the proletarian party should in words and in deeds openly and boldly take the solution of the national (racial) problem in its hands. . . .

When the thesis says that the slogan of a "Black Republic" is *equally* harmful for the revolutionary cause as is the slogan of a

"South Africa for the Whites," then we cannot agree with the form of the statement. Whereas in the latter there is the case of supporting complete oppression, in the former there is the case of taking the first steps toward liberation.

We must accept decisively and without any reservation the complete and unconditional right of the blacks to independence. Only on the basis of a mutual struggle against the domination of the white exploiters can the solidarity of black and white toilers be cultivated and strengthened.

It is possible that *after* victory the blacks will find it unnecessary to form a separate black state in South Africa. Certainly we will not *force them* to establish a separate state. But let them make this decision freely, on the basis of their own experience, and not forced by the *sjambok* [whip] of the white oppressors. The proletarian revolutionaries must never forget the right of the oppressed nationalities to self-determination, including full separation, and the duty of the proletariat of the oppressing nation to defend this right with arms in hand if necessary. . . .

The worst crime on the part of the revolutionaries would be to give the smallest concessions to the privileges and prejudices of the whites. Whoever gives his little finger to the devil of chauvinism is lost.

The revolutionary party must put before every white worker the following alternative: either with British imperialism and with the white bourgeoisie of South Africa, or with the black workers and peasants against the white feudalists and slave-owners and their agents in the ranks of the working class.

> "On the South African Theses," April 20, 1935,
> reprinted in *Writings of Leon Trotsky (1934-35)*

The Movement of the Colored Races

In a preface to the first translation into Afrikaans of The Communist Manifesto, *written on the* Manifesto's *ninetieth anniversary, Trotsky pointed out why in that document Marx and Engels had not dealt with the questions of revolutionary strategy by op-*

pressed nationalities and colonial or semicolonial countries. Then he added:

"The Communists," declares the *Manifesto,* "everywhere support every revolutionary movement against the existing social and political order of things." The movement of the colored races against their imperialist oppressors is one of the most important and powerful movements against the existing order and therefore calls for the complete, unconditional, and unlimited support on the part of the proletariat of the white race. The credit for developing revolutionary strategy for oppressed nationalities belongs primarily to Lenin.

> "Ninety Years of the Communist Manifesto,"
> October 30, 1937, reprinted in
> *Writings of Leon Trotsky (1937-38)*

The Slave-Owners and the Slave

Trotsky despised those who told slaves that it was wrong to use any means necessary to free themselves:

We leave to some Emil Ludwig or his ilk the drawing of Abraham Lincoln's portrait with rosy little wings. Lincoln's significance lies in his not hesitating before the most severe means, once they were found to be necessary, in achieving a great historic aim posed by the development of a young nation. The question lies not even in which of the warring camps caused or itself suffered the greatest number of victims. History has different yardsticks for the cruelty of the Northerners and the cruelty of the Southerners in the Civil War. A slave-owner who through cunning and violence shackles a slave in chains, and a slave who through cunning or violence breaks the chains—let not the contemptible eunuchs tell us that they are equals before a court of morality!

> "Their Morals and Ours," February 16, 1938,
> reprinted in *Their Morals and Ours*

In Defense of the Kaffirs

A German emigré newspaper, Neuer Weg *(The New Road), had condemned the "Bolshevik amoralism" of Lenin and Trotsky. "We should free ourselves," it declared, "from those morals of the Kaffirs to whom only what the enemy does is wrong." Trotsky wrote:*

To apply different criteria to the actions of the exploiters and the exploited signifies, according to these pitiful mannikins, standing on the level of the "morals of the Kaffirs." First of all such a contemptuous reference to the Kaffirs is hardly proper from the pen of "socialists." Are the morals of the Kaffirs really so bad? Here is what the *Encyclopedia Britannica* says upon the subject:

"In their social and political relations they display great tact and intelligence; they are remarkably brave, warlike and hospitable, and were honest and truthful until through contact with the whites they became suspicious, revengeful and thievish, besides acquiring most European vices." It is impossible not to arrive at the conclusion that white missionaries, preachers of eternal morals, participated in the corruption of the Kaffirs.

If we should tell the toiler-Kaffir how the workers arose in a part of our planet and caught their exploiters unawares, he would be very pleased. On the other hand, he would be chagrined to discover that the oppressors had succeeded in deceiving the oppressed. A Kaffir who has not been demoralized by missionaries to the marrow of his bones will never apply the selfsame abstract moral norms to the oppressors and the oppressed. Yet he will easily comprehend an explanation that it is the function of these abstract norms to prevent the oppressed from arising against their oppressors.

What an instructive coincidence! In order to slander the Bolsheviks, the missionaries of *Neuer Weg* were compelled at the same time to slander the Kaffirs; moreover in both cases the slander follows the line of the official bourgeois lie: against revolutionists and against the colored races. No, we prefer the Kaffirs to all missionaries, both spiritual and secular!

"Their Morals and Ours," February 16, 1938,
reprinted in *Their Morals and Ours*

To Him Who Helps Himself

Trotsky categorically rejected the idea that oppressed peoples should "wait" for the workers in the industrially advanced countries before striking out with revolutionary struggle on their own. In his last programmatic document, written early in World War II, he said:

Only under its own revolutionary direction is the proletariat of the colonies and the semicolonies capable of achieving invincible collaboration with the proletariat of the metropolitan centers and with the world working class as a whole. Only this can lead the oppressed peoples to complete and final emancipation, through the overthrow of imperialism the world over. A victory of the international proletariat will deliver the colonial countries from the long drawn-out travail of capitalist development by opening up the possibility of arriving at socialism hand in hand with the proletariat of the advanced countries.

The perspective of permanent revolution in no case signifies that the backward countries must await the signal from the advanced ones, or that the colonial peoples should patiently wait for the proletariat of the metropolitan centers to free them. Help comes to him who helps himself. Workers must develop the revolutionary struggle in every country, colonial or imperialist, where favorable conditions have been established, and through this set an example for the workers of other countries. Only initiative and activity, resoluteness and boldness can give reality to the call, "Workers of the world, unite!"

"Manifesto of the Fourth International on the
Imperialist War and the Proletarian Revolution,"
reprinted in *Writings of Leon Trotsky (1939-40)*

For Self-Determination in Workers' States

*Trotsky's-defense of the right of self-determination was not re-
stricted to nations oppressed by imperialism; it was also applied
to nations oppressed by a workers' state. In 1939 he advocated an
independent Soviet Ukraine and gave the following answer to the
objections of a sectarian critic (Hugo Oehler):*

If our critic were capable of thinking politically, he would have
surmised without much difficulty the arguments of the Stalinists
against the slogan of an independent Ukraine: "It negates the
position of the defense of the Soviet Union"; "disrupts the unity
of the revolutionary masses"; "serves not the interests of revolution but those of imperialism." In other words, the Stalinists
would repeat all the three arguments of our author. They will un-
failingly do so on the morrow.

The Kremlin bureaucracy tells the Soviet woman: Inasmuch as
there is socialism in our country, you must be happy and you
must give up abortions (or suffer the penalty). To the Ukrainian
they say: Inasmuch as the socialist revolution has solved the national question, it is your duty to be happy in the USSR and to
renounce all thought of separation (or face the firing squad).

What does a revolutionist say to the woman? "You will decide
yourself whether you want a child; I will defend your right to
abortion against the Kremlin police." To the Ukrainian people he
says: "Of importance to me is your attitude toward your national
destiny and not the 'socialistic' sophistries of the Kremlin police;
I will support your struggle for independence with all my might!"

The sectarian, as so often happens, finds himself siding with
the police, covering up the status quo, that is, police violence, by
sterile speculation on the superiority of the socialist unification of
nations as against their remaining divided. Assuredly, the separation of the Ukraine is a liability as compared with a voluntary
and equalitarian socialist federation: but it will be an unquestion-
able asset as compared with the bureaucratic strangulation of the
Ukrainian people. In order to draw together more closely and
honestly, it is sometimes necessary first to separate. Lenin often
used to cite the fact that the relations between the Norwegian and

Swedish workers improved and became closer after the disruption of the compulsory unification of Sweden and Norway.

"Independence of the Ukraine and Sectarian Muddleheads," July 30, 1939, reprinted in *Writings of Leon Trotsky (1939-40)*

For Every Lynching

Talking with leaders of the Socialist Workers Party in June 1940, after an unsuccessful attempt to assassinate him, Trotsky said:

The white slaveholders accustom the Negroes not to speak first. But on the picket line they show more courage. That is true of all oppressed nationalities. We must approach them everywhere by advocating that for every lynching they should lynch ten or twenty lynchers.

"Discussions with Trotsky," June 15, 1940, reprinted in *Writings of Leon Trotsky (1939-40)*

Index

BOOKS AND PAMPHLETS BY LEON TROTSKY*

Against Individual Terrorism
The Age of Permanent Revolution
The Basic Writings of Trotsky
Between Red and White
The Bolsheviki and World Peace
(War and the International)
The Case of Leon Trotsky
The Challenge of the Left Opposition (1923-25) (incl. The New Course, Lessons of October, Problems of Civil War, and Toward Socialism or Capitalism?)
The Crisis of the French Section (1935-36)
Europe and America: Two Speeches on Imperialism
Fascism: What It Is and How to Fight It
The First Five Years of the Communist International (2 vols.)
The History of the Russian Revolution (3 vols.)
In Defense of Marxism
Lenin: Notes for a Biographer
Lenin's Fight Against Stalinism (with V.I. Lenin)
Leon Trotsky Speaks
Literature and Revolution
Marxism in Our Time
Military Writings
My Life
1905
On Black Nationalism and Self-Determination
On Britain (incl. Where Is Britain Going?)
On China (incl. Problems of the Chinese Revolution)
On the Jewish Question
On Literature and Art

On the Paris Commune
On the Trade Unions
Our Revolution
The Permanent Revolution and Results and Prospects
Portraits, Political and Personal
Problems of Everyday Life and Other Writings on Culture and Science
The Revolution Betrayed
The Spanish Revolution (1931-39)
Stalin
The Stalin School of Falsification
The Struggle Against Fascism in Germany
Terrorism and Communism
Their Morals and Ours (with essays by John Dewey and George Novack)
The Third International After Lenin
The Transitional Program for Socialist Revolution (incl. The Death Agony of Capitalism and the Tasks of the Fourth International)
Trotsky's Diary in Exile, 1935
Women and the Family
Writings of Leon Trotsky (1929-40) (12 vols.)
The Young Lenin

In preparation:
The Challenge of the Left Opposition (1926-29) (incl. The Platform of the Opposition)
Kronstadt (with V.I. Lenin)
On France (incl. Whither France?)
The War Correspondence of Leon Trotsky

---

*This list includes only books and pamphlets by Leon Trotsky published in the United States and in print as of 1978.